The INFLUENCE *of* LEADERSHIP

"The charismatic portrait of modern leadership looks nothing like Fidel Castro. It is a faceless portrait that epitomizes the toughness of Ronald Reagan, Nelson Mandela's charisma, and the most compassionate heart of Mother Theresa."

Dr. Anthony Obi Ogbo

A phenomenological study of the influence of Nigerian leadership on the life of its citizens

By

Dr. Anthony Obi Ogbo

Study Supervision

Ogwo J. Umeh, PhD

Elizabeth Young, PhD

Chizoba Madueke, PhD

School of Advanced Studies
University of Phoenix

American Journal of Transformational Leadership

ProQuest Dissertations
ProQuest Databases

Texas International
Guardian, Inc.

Texas International Guardian Newspapers Inc.

CreateSpace Independent Publishing Platform.
ISBN-13: 978-1515238270
ISBN-10: 151523827X
Printed in the United States of America (USA).

Cover design, book design, and production *by*
Anthony Obi Ogbo, *International Guardian*

This book is a reproduction of studies based on a Dissertation presented Anthony Obi Ogbo in partial fulfillment of the requirements for the degree Doctor of Management in Organizational Leadership

Research Study Supervision

Dr. Ogwo J. Umeh, PhD
Elizabeth Young, PhD
Chizoba Madueke, PhD

Research Study Approval

Jeremy Moreland, PhD
Dean, School of Advanced Studies,
University of Phoenix

DEDICATION

I dedicate this book to my late parents, Fidelis and Cecelia Ogbo who deprived themselves of earthly treats and luxuries to support and motivate their eight children through college education.

APPRECIATION

It 'takes a village,' and special thanks must go to both the seen and unseen individuals that have contributed in various ways to make this publication possible; Dr. Chris Ulasi, Dr. Emeaba Emeaba, Dr. Charles Nwankwo, Joe Nwokedi, Dr. Rita Kingsley, Dr. Anthony Kingsley, Chief Chris Ogbo, Paul Nwokedi, Stephanie Adaeze Ogbo, Anthony Obieze Ogbo, Isaac Chibueze Ogbo, Chief Uzo and Lady Laura Ekume, Chief Okwie and Lady May Oraelosi; editorial staff of *International Guardian*, and *The Guardian News Network.*

For developing my competencies in Management in Organizational Leadership, special appreciation to the Doctoral Community at the University of Phoenix, especially; my mentors, Dr. Ogwo J. Umeh, Dr. Elizabeth Young, and Dr. Chizoba Madueke for the round-the-clock support of my dissertation project. Going through this process with your supervision and support impelled my enthusiasm and drove my motivation to the finishing line.

My doctoral experience was a successful long journey made possible by a thread of other able professors at the University of Phoenix. My special appreciation goes to all my doctoral student instructors, namely: Manuel Ferreira (Doctoral Success Orientation), Linda De Charon (Communication Strategies), Jean Perlman (Doctoral Program Orientation Seminar), Jane Armstrong (Leadership Theory and Practice), Andrew Edelman (Creative and Critical Thinking), Jerry Dibble (Knowledge of Theory and Practice), Michael Mc Intyre (Constructing Meaning), Sushil Jindal (Fundamental Principles of Sound Research), Xianbin Li (Research Design), Gregory Berry (Organizational Theory and Design), Ruby Daniels (Doctoral Seminar I), Meredith Ward (Management Philosophies), Amy Preiss (The Dynamics of Group and Team Leadership), Holly Rick (The Impact of Technology on Organizations), Timothy Clifton (The Impact of Technology on Organizations), Ogwo Umeh (Doctoral Seminar II; Doctoral Dissertation), Lee Burnham (Collaborative Case Study), Elizabeth Young (Doctoral Seminar III), Richard De Paris (Organizational Diagnosis and Intervention), Jonathan Mc Govern (Political Acumen and Ethics), Betty Ahmed (Contemporary Systems Management), Robert Johnson (Architecture of Leadership).

-Dr. Anthony Obi Ogbo

ABSTRACT

Complexities of Nigeria's leadership exacerbated major problems influencing citizens' experience of livelihood. Amidst surmounting socio-political challenges, a lack of effective leadership provoked extraordinary social problems. The purpose of the qualitative phenomenological research study was to understand how political, cultural, social and economic conditions in Nigeria influence the lives of Nigerian citizens through lived experiences of citizens from each of the six geopolitical regions of the country namely, North-Central, North-Eastern, North-Western, South-Eastern, South-South, and South-Western regions. The general problem was that the quality of life that the citizens of the country experience was dependent on the leadership and when the leadership is flawed, the citizens may suffer. The study provided an insightful understanding of the experiences of Nigerians experiencing the consequences of a leadership process by exploring the fundamental research question: How do Nigerian citizens describe their experience of living under economic, political, cultural, and social hardships? The study was guided by a theoretical framework that included

ABSTRACT

Fred Fielder's Contingency Leadership theory, Transactional, and Transformational Leadership theories. The study exclusively used semi-unstructured interviews to gather relevant data. Interview transcription were systematically coded with Nvivo 10® software and analyzed with Moustakas' (1994) modified van Kaam data analysis method. Themes identified included: moral philosophy, skills and training, ineffective management, and politics and diversity. Recommendations made for leaders to inspire effective management in organizational leadership consisted of moral philosophy, organizational change, transformation, and diversity management. Future studies may validate the current findings by carrying out similar research in other countries or geographical areas.

Table of Contents

LIST OF TABLES

LIST OF FIGURES

Chapter 1
Introduction

■ General George Patton's avowal that one can either lead, follow, or get out of the way (Patton, 1978, 1947) dovetails the classification of leadership theory and research through three relevant elements; leaders, followers, and the situation (Yukl, 2013).

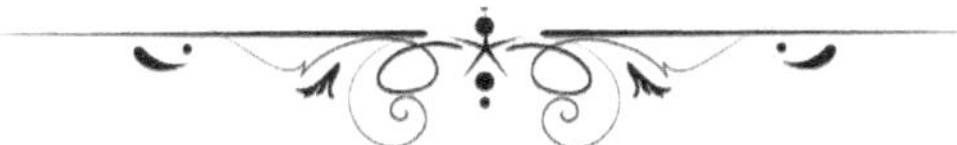

Leading does not only involve organizing and inspiring the masses for greater productivity but also entails managing them with well-defined objectives (Stogdill, 1948). Leadership is not a birthmark; it is an intricate observable fact involving the constant interaction of three essential elements: the leaders, the followers, and the surrounding situation and context (Bass & Avolio; Bass, 1990; Burns, 1978; Vroom & Yetton, 1973; Yukl, 2013; Wren, 1995). According to Clawson (2006), leadership entails the dynamics of managing or influencing people – which is a justification that before any one initiates the ambition to influence others, he must think and reflect on the rules, structures, and complexities of management. These definitions and thoughts have also been replicated in words and actions by great leaders of the times. For instance, General George Patton's avowal that one can either lead, follow, or get out of the way (Patton, 1978, 1947) dovetails the classification of leadership theory and research through three relevant elements; leaders, followers, and the situation (Yukl, 2013). These reflections and works of remarkable leadership theorists including, Stogdill, Bass, Burns, and Vroom set the stage for the current dissertation topic and introduce a rationale for the exploration of the influence of Nigerian leadership on the quality of life of its citizens. This phenomenological investigation focused on descriptions of the citizens' experience and generated findings that revealed relevant elements that contributed potentially to flaws in the Nigerian government.

Complexity and conflicts in Nigeria's leadership process, past and present has been undisputable (Rice, 1998; Achebe, 2003; Kehinde, 2009; Polgreen, 2007; 2009; Agbiboa, 2010; Ezimma, 2010; Odion & Omolere, 2011; Joseph, 2012; Lawal, Imokhuede, & Johnson, 2012; Abdullahi, Yahya, & Yelwa, 2012; Idris, 2013). In the midst of surmounting socio-political challenges, Nigeria's potentials as a regional powerhouse remain realistic as this country inhabits a population of over 152 million people, with 250 ethnic groups; parades a wealth of natural resources, and has the largest domestic market in the continent (Nigeria, 2011). The country remains influential and large; endowed with ancient culture, outstanding human talent, vast prosperity, and democratic competency (Rice, 1998). Since its attainment of independence from Britain in 1960, the nation has not been endowed with sufficient leadership. This perception corroborated a conclusion that from the first democratic experience in 1960, Nigeria has struggled from civilian to military regimes, and has been ruled by self-centered leaders who amass wealth at tax-payers' expense without commitment to the people they represent (Agbiboa, 2010; Ezimma, 2010).

Under the perception that leadership is a fundamental element for the accomplishment of any nation's building and development, Adegboyega (2013) argued that effective service-oriented leadership is the primary reason why the government of Nigeria is developing at a very slow pace. Studies by Idris, (2013); Olu-Adeyemi (2012); Lawal, Imokhuede, and Johnson (2012), and Ezimma (2010) have linked Nigeria's governance failure to ethical lapses, citing corruption, indiscipline, and dishonesty among public officials as the problems of a lack of effective leadership. Reliable international rating institutions have also consistently confirmed Nigeria's governance catastrophe with outrageous ratings on ethics. Nigeria has repeatedly been categorized as one of the three most unethical nations in the world by Transparency International and this situation has been worsened by leaders with little or no regards for the ordinary man (Agbiboa, 2010). For instance, between 1960 and 1999, more than $440 billion had been embezzled by Nigerian public servants: six times the total amount needed to rebuild Europe after a shattering Second World War (Agbiboa, 2010).

Chapter 1 of this study started with a synopsis of the study's content, followed by a narrative of the general problem. Within this chapter, the specific problem statement, and the purpose statements are explained to justify the study, its implications in Nigeria's governance, and the study of management in organizational leadership. The chapter substantiates the significance of the study by investigating theories which increase understanding of the leadership process, dynamics, and functioning factors as they correlate the social, political, cultural, and economic development of Nigeria. Vast discussions about relevant theories are articulated as a foundation for this study whereas some commonly used terminologies are defined for clarification and comprehensibility. Chapter One also includes discussions on the evaluation of the study's fundamental expectations, scope, limitations, delimitations, and a brief introduction of Chapter Two.

Background of the Problem

The problem with Nigeria is basically and exactly a miscarriage of leadership, wrote a Nobel Laureate Chinua Achebe (1983) in his infamous book *The Trouble with Nigeria.* There is nothing intrinsically wrong with the Nigerian character. There is nothing wrong with this country except the leaders: their unwillingness to rise up to expectation, and inability to shoulder the crucial test of leadership by example, all of which are the dividends of actual governance (Achebe, 1983). A skyrocketing prevalence of the wrath of bad leaders in the form of insecurity and corruption in Nigeria constitutes a pronounced leadership challenge and has thus become matters of unbearable public worries (Idris, 2013). The purpose of the qualitative phenomenological research study was to understand how political, cultural, social and economic conditions in Nigeria influence the lives of Nigerian citizens through lived experiences of two citizens from each of the six geopolitical regions of the country namely, North-Central, North-Eastern, North-Western, South-Eastern, South-South, and South-Western regions. Whereas observers and analysts in various journals have addressed several subjects on this issue, the question arises about how Nigerian citizens describe their experience of living under economic, political, cultural, and social hardships?

Since her independence in 1960, political leadership in Nigeria has been riddled with uncertainty. The country was governed for thirty-five years out of fifty-four years by the military. The military governments have presided with an iron fist under misguided policies, mismanagement, and corruption (Rice, 1998). The military governments imposed scores of obstacles to restrict the democratic process, outlawing political parties, and banning Politicians from politics for inexplicable intentions (Rotimi & Ihonvbere, 1994). Violence has become a veritable tool in the mindless struggle to "control" politics by the elites (Kehinde, 2009). The leadership of Nigeria in every regime (civilian or military) has criminally mismanaged the country's affairs and resources (Joseph, 2012). Consistent conflicts over ethnic and religious differences remain cancerous not only in the country's attainment of true democracy, but also in its existence as a sovereign entity (Mercy, 2012).

The leadership election process has been hijacked by individuals who have organized themselves into a cabal with the ultimate goal of determining the pace of political choices and structures in their regions (Odion & Omolere, 2011). They display a catastrophic mix of fraud and ignorance in undermining the electoral structure (Polgreen, 2007). Democracy has also been a major casualty of Nigeria's leadership woes, and a lack of democratic values has ignited political intolerance, barbarism, electoral rigging, constitutional juggling, and outright rule-breaking (Kehinde, 2009). Since achieving independence in 1960, Nigeria has only produced the caliber of leaders who somehow lack vision, or are enthralled by corruption and governmental wrangling. These shortfalls have thrown the nation into an administrative catastrophe, economic maladministration, and social deprivation (Lawal, Imokhuede, & Johnson, 2012).

To further emphasize the magnitude of Nigeria's leadership cataclysm, Ezimma (2010) corroborated reports of repeated upsurges in bribery, misappropriation of funds, extortion and self- embellishment among affluent and powerful Nigerians in corridors of power. This situation prompted the enactment of various regulations by national agencies authorized to address the problems. Research literature explicitly addressed the experience of Nigerians living under a leadership flawed by economic, political, cultural, and social hardships. This qualitative phenomenological research study was conducted to add new information to existing knowledge of the practice of management in organizational leadership behaviors and approaches of the Nigerian governmental system. The projected knowledge might help to increase the development of more effective leaders in Nigeria.

Problem Statement

On the complex nature of leading, Burns (1978) noted that leadership as a phenomenon is enormously observed but least understood. The lack of effective leadership in Nigeria has created extraordinary social problems unbearable to the citizens who now seek greener pastures in other countries (Odunsi, 1996). The general problem addressed in this study was that the quality of life that the citizens of a country experience was dependent on the leadership and when the leadership is flawed, the citizens may suffer (Odunsi, 1996; Abdullahi, Yahya, & Yelwa, 2012; Lawal, Imokhuede, & Johnson, 2012; Ojo, Ugochukwu, & Obinna, 2011; Ebegbulem, 2012; Agbiboa, 2012). Nigeria is a country endowed with enough natural resources to boost its economic and sociopolitical management, yet citizens suffer from economic deprivation (Lawal, Imokhuede, & Johnson, 2012). The need to develop relevant leadership knowledge in the Nigerian governmental system receives little or no attention (Lawal, Imokhuede, & Johnson, 2012). The specific problem under study is that the Nigerian leadership was flawed and exacerbates the political, economic, cultural and social problems which directly influence the way citizens experience livelihood (Abdullahi, Yahya, & Yelwa, 2012).

Consistent conflicts over ethnic and religious differences remain cancerous not only in the country's attainment of true democracy, but also in its existence as a sovereign entity (Mercy, 2012). Bad leadership has cost the Nigerian government the migration to foreign countries, an extremely skilled manpower made up of talented professionals who are saddened by insufficient economic rewards, and unfavorable work condition (Ojo, Ugochukwu, & Obinna, 2011). The outflow of skilled professionals attributed to a flawed leadership has adversely affected Nigeria's socio-political progress. This has significantly affected efforts at human resource mobilization for economic development and consequently eroded Nigeria's leadership role in Africa despite its enormous population (Odunsi, 1996).

Purpose Statement

The purpose of the qualitative phenomenological research study was to understand how political, cultural, social and economic conditions in Nigeria influence the lives of Nigerian citizens through lived experiences of two citizens from each of the six geopolitical regions of the country namely, North-Central, North-Eastern, North-Western, South-Eastern, South-South, and South-Western regions. Using semi-structured interviews and open-ended questions, the current study used Moustakas (1994) modified van Kaam data-analysis technique to facilitate 12 Nigerian citizens, who shared in their own words, their individual experience of living under a leadership condition flawed by economic, political, cultural, and social hardships (Odunsi, 1996; Abdullahi, Yahya, & Yelwa, 2012).

The current study was accomplished through existential phenomenological methodology because the study examiner focused more on participant's experiences and actions rather than dwelled on conventionality or behavior (Moustakas, 1994). Phenomenological researchers aim at describing what research participants have in common as they experience an event (Moustakas, 1994; Kvale, 1996). Using Moustakas (1994) modified van Kaam method of analysis, the research design was performed through semi-structured interviews of 12 Nigerians drawn from two organizations; (1) visiting citizens who attend monthly meetings of Organization 'A' (Org. A), and (2) visiting citizens who attend monthly meetings of the Organization 'B' (Org. B). They are both locally-based international professional organizations in the United States labelled Org. A and Org. B for confidentiality. In the process, participants were asked to describe their experiences of living under a system flawed by economic, political, cultural, and social hardships (Lawal, Imokhuede, & Johnson, 2012). The study examiner developed a combined description of the essential aspects of the phenomenon as experienced by all of the participants, focusing on the events they lived through and in the manner they experienced it (Moustakas, 1994).

The dividends of leadership styles have not been adequately exploited in Nigeria's governance process (Odunsi, 1996). Leaders have not explored specific leadership styles strongly associated with performance effectiveness and success (Odunsi, 1996; Abdullahi, Yahya, & Yelwa, 2012). The outcome of this study revealed and highlighted fundamental factors contributing to Nigeria's leadership flaws and specific reasons the leadership processes have been troubled since its independence in 1960 (Odunsi, 1996). Other findings revealed a better knowledge about leadership styles, behaviors, and performances, and could enable Nigerian leaders seek alternative approaches to effective leadership.

Significance of Study to Management

The current study is essential to existing research because it revealed an insightful understanding of Nigeria's management process, the underperformances, and implications. It added new information to existing knowledge of the practice of management in organizational leadership, and structures of the Nigerian governmental system. This knowledge might help to increase the development of more effective leaders in

Nigeria. It has been argued extensively that the main problem that has grounded Nigeria as well as intensified its socio-economic, and political problems is poor leadership and corruption (Ebegbulem, 2012; Achebe, 2003). Agbiboa (2012) attributed persistent sociopolitical problems in Nigeria to a communal fragmentation, imbalanced governmental structure, and fruitless political culture.

Amidst a rise in poverty level, a prolonged leadership uncertainty and the economic maladministration reflect the broad sociopolitical problems that derail progress (The Economist Intelligence Unit, 2012; Agbiboa, 2012). As noted by Ebegbulem (2012), because of mismanagement, the leaders produced by this country, thus far, have blighted the lives of the citizens who now struggle without basic public amenities. The aforementioned problem analysis is a revelation that Nigeria has suffered adversely from the devastation imposed by economic deprivation and human resource imbalance since its independence in 1960 (Odunsi, 1996).

Studies have pondered how despite Nigeria's enormous oil prosperity and indeed its rank as the world's eighth largest oil producer, the country subsists in poverty and is unable to provide basic amenities to its citizen. Studies by Agbiboa, (2010) substantiated the link between corruption and underdevelopment, and blamed the inadequacies and a lack of performance of the Nigerian political economy on corrupt and irresponsible leaders. The current study offered substantial insights about Nigeria's leadership flaws and raised awareness regarding the relevance of studies of management. Through this study, Nigerian leaders might become better informed about theories of organizational leadership as performance development tools and strategies. This study also added to the body of knowledge in the literature about the role and influence of Nigerian leadership structures on the quality of life of its citizens.

Significance of Study

By exploring lived experiences of Nigerian citizens under the influence of political, cultural, social and economic conditions, new knowledge on effective leadership was provided. Knowledge acquired could add to the existing literature to expand studies on leadership effectiveness. With hundreds of journals and dissertations scattered in various academic catalogs addressing issues of Nigeria's governance cataclysm, the outcome of this study may further develop the scope of organizational leadership with constructive educational values. It might create avenues for scholarly discussions on the approach and application of leadership models in the realms of governmental complexities.

Present day leaders and organizations must be prepared to face the demands of a new era of competitiveness and persistent innovation (Moseley & Dessinger, 2010; Scott & Davis, 2007; Brown, 2011). It is imperative that most successful organizations are those that respond quickly to the needs and the changing aspirations of the masses. To live up to this anticipation, successful organizations would rely on effective strategies of management in organizational leadership to meet citizens' expectation (Bass, Jung, Avolio, & Berson, 2003). By studying lived experiences of Nigerian citizens living through a governance phenomenon, findings, could strategically help the present and future leaders in countries struggling with resources management to direct a constructive performance intervention of startling governance anguishes.

Other findings might offer substantial information in the studies of management in organizational leadership, and create opportunities for upcoming research.

Nature of the Study

A qualitative study identifies disparities in existing knowledge and research about a specific issue or topic, thus validating the need for adequate reporting. Researchers provide a detailed description of situations they have studied. The nature of any qualitative research study has fundamental components. It is interpretive; the researcher continually handles data from the participants' subjective perspectives, and the process tends to be most useful for creating theories (Patton, 2002). The purpose of the qualitative phenomenological research study was to understand how political, cultural, social, and economic conditions in Nigeria influence the lives of Nigerian citizens through lived experiences of two citizens from each of the six geopolitical regions of the country namely, North-Central, North-Eastern, North-Western, South-Eastern, South-South, and South-Western regions. Drawing samples from each of the geopolitical zones increases the validity of the study in ensuring that findings are an accurate representation of the phenomena. The study aimed at capturing the lived experiences of the study participants by engaging them in complex situations and interactions (Moustakas, 1994).

A qualitative study was appropriate for the current study because the process involve an in-depth exploration of the phenomenon for people who are experiencing the issues (Moustakas, 1994; Patton, 1990). The process also examine people's observations, comprehension, and perspectives on a specific circumstance (Moustakas 1994). Existential phenomenological method was appropriate and enabled an investigation of participants' feelings and experiences about the phenomenon as they appear (Moustakas, 1994). In existential phenomenology, the researcher focuses on problems being experienced by citizens in daily living (van Manen, 1990). Under the study method, participants were allowed in all conscience, to describe their feelings about the phenomenon as they appeared. Under this setting, the quantitative approach which is processed by testing theories, measuring numbers, and analyzing statistical methods would have been inappropriate (Babbie, 2001; Jencik, 2011). Furthermore, the Mixed Research method was not considered for this study because a combination of testing and generation of hypothesis or theory was not relevant.

Researchers seeking qualitative studies can also use other standard methods such as case study, ethnography, and grounded theory. However, these approaches possess specific attributes that are incompatible with the purpose of the current phenomenological study. For instance, case study would not have been appropriate in the current research because the process relies on observations, documents, interviews, and other data generated by several sources to examine the issue. The case study method uses a specific location and last over a period (Richards and Morse, 2007). The qualitative ethnography would not have been inappropriate for the current study because the process describes the characteristics of a culture through close observations, readings, and interpretations. Ethnographers gain entrance to participants' culture to facilitate necessary observation and interaction to gather data (Miles & Huberman, 1994). Grounded theory focuses on developing a theory about the process for where existing theories are insufficient. In a grounded theory, researchers concentrate on generating theories from data consisting of inductive and deductive thinking, and explain the workings of some aspect of the social world (Strauss & Corbin, 1998).

Study participants served as a primary data source in the current research study. The research examiner employed a qualitative existential phenomenological method to gain insight into the lived experience of each participant (Moustakas, 1994). The process involved conducting interviews with 12 participants drawn from visiting Nigerians citizens who attend monthly meetings of two organizations labelled as Org. A and Org. B respectively. Both groups are locally based and are structurally diverse with visiting Nigerians from different geopolitical regions. The organizations currently host visiting Nigerian citizens to monthly community meetings. An applicable sample size for a qualitative study should satisfactorily provide answers to the research question. A distinctive sample size is from five to twenty-five interviewees with direct experience with the research subject (Marshall, 1996). The interview process must establish and construct the interviewee's experience, and that the composition must reflect the meaning (van Manen, 1990; Moustakas, 1994; Seidman, 1991; Maxwell, 2005). The study relied exclusively on extensive semi-unstructured interviews to gather relevant data. Open-ended and exploratory questions was posed to each study participant in a flexible set-up that allowed them to give accounts individually in their words (Moustakas, 1994). For instance, participants were asked through interview questions as shown in Appendix D, to describe their experiences of living under a system under exploration (van Manen, 1990).

For process expediency and accuracy, Moustakas (1994) recommended an audio recording of interviews in combination with taking necessary notes in writing. Consent Forms were handed over to the individuals who agreed to take part in the study. The interview proceeded after the consent forms were signed and received. During the interview process, the researcher set aside any prejudgments in a process known as epoché (Moustakas, 1994; van Manen, 1990). Epoché is a process whereby the researcher sets aside personal experiences or knowledge of the studied phenomenon from an entirely new perspective (van Manen, 1990). Notes taken during the interview session with individual participants were systematically transcribed and entered into Nvivo 10® software for processing and data-coding. Final data input were systematically analyzed through the modified van Kaam data analysis method by Moustakas (1994).

Research Question

Qualitative research questions are very significant, and constitute one of the first major steps in the research process. As stated by Moustakas (1994), qualitative research questions are open-ended researchable questions that the researcher intends to explore during the study. These questions take shape from the initial topic and guide the research study. According to Moustakas (1994), research questions should be composed with significant features that must include:

1. Identifying the central phenomenon of the planned study.
2. Identifying the study participants and the research site.
3. Revealing the essence of the participant's experience.
4. Desisting from suggesting a possible cause-effect con-

nection.

The current study offered an insightful understanding of Nigerians experiencing living under the consequences of a leadership system by exploring the fundamental research question: How do Nigerian citizens describe their experience of living under economic, political, cultural, and social hardships? The question was directed to a phenomenological study to explore the influence of political, economic, cultural, and social influences in the lives of the citizens living in the Nigerian system. The study used extensive interviews with citizens living in the six Nigerian geopolitical regions and other relevant literatures to corroborate new understanding about how citizens experience living under a prevalent leadership. Study participants discussed their observations and experiences of the leaders, events, and related policies. The research question directed the current qualitative study and helped to reveal effective leadership behavior and practices to improve the lives of Nigerian citizens.

Theoretical Framework

In the modern era of transformation and innovative leadership, Tichy and Devanna (1990) classify a leader as transformational and prudent risk-takers who directs risky, innovative solutions involving unexpected outcomes. Such a leader must inspire change, motivate subordinates and carry them along toward the finishing line (Kotter, 2012). One of the keys to an organization's long-term success lies in the ability of the leaders to face imminent challenges. This medium would entail developing a clear vision, supporting organizational structure of innovation, and commitment to a strategic plan for performance accomplishment (Yukl, 2013; Nahavandi, 2012). To meet such challenges, leaders must be equipped with transformational individuality, including personality values, confidence, expertise, influence tactic, and relevant behaviors (Yukl, 2013).

The purpose of the qualitative phenomenological research study was to understand how political, cultural, social, and economic conditions in Nigeria influence the lives of Nigerian citizens through lived experiences of two citizens from each of the six geopolitical regions of the country namely, North-Central, North-Eastern, North-Western, South-Eastern, South-South, and South-Western regions. To develop a new knowledge about this purpose, applicable leadership theories were reviewed in relation to the leaders, and the citizens currently experiencing the phenomena. Theories can be expressed to explicate, forecast, and understand a phenomenon; they can be explained to challenge and enlarge existing knowledge within the boundaries of vital assumptions (Maxwell, 2009). The theoretical framework in the current research study presented and explained theories justifying the existence of the research problem under study.

Throughout several centuries, fundamental leadership theories have survived and made tremendous impacts in several ways. However, the demands of the current era often contradict some common suppositions of the past. A comprehensive review of the existing literature progressed to a consideration of relevant leadership theories namely; Fred Fielder's Contingency Leadership theory (Fiedler, 1967), Transactional, and Transformational Leadership theories (Burns, 1978; Bass, 1990). These theories guided the framework for the current qualitative phenomenological study.

Conceptually, there is a major correlation between leadership styles, behavioral styles, and followership (Chaleff, 1995; Kellerman, 1984; Burns, 1978), thus leadership and behavioral styles determine the quality of life of the citizens. By exploring how Nigeria's leadership influence the lives of citizens, the current study reviewed traits associated with aforementioned leadership theories as study's conceptual frameworks (Yukl, 2013). Concepts associated with Fiedler's contingency theory entail leader-followership rapport, task structure, and position power (Fiedler, 2006; Stogdill). Transformational theory encompasses idealized influence, inspirational motivation, intellectual motivation, intellectual stimulation, and individualized consideration (Bass, 1990; Bass & Avolio, 1990). Transactional theory involve three behavioral styles of leadership, namely; Contingent Reward (CR) and Active Management by Exception (AMBE), and Passive Management by Exception (PMBE) (Bass, 1990; Bass & Avolio, 1990).

Fiedler's contingency theory assumes that applicable leadership style is dependent on the prevailing situation. The process regulates situational context to match styles rather than making routine changes (Fiedler, 2006; Stogdill, 1995; Chemers, 1997). For instance, in a mechanistic task-based labor environment, a moderately instructional approach might yield efficient performance, whereas a lively situation might necessitate a participative process (Stogdill, 1995). The contingency leadership theory characterizes several fundamental implications that correlate the study purpose as conceptual frameworks (Fiedler, 2006; Stogdill, 1995):

1. The leader-followership approach encourages sheer relationship between the leaders and the followers.
2. The task process emphasizes the nature of tasks.
3. Position power prioritizes the nature of leaders' athority

Transformational leaders encourage followers to accomplish goals beyond personal interests. They create avenues for opportunities and stimulate followers to solving problems. In the transformational setting, leaders elevate the followers with motivating and charismatic qualities. The followers only identify with the leadership because the rules, guidelines, and other governance attributes are flexible and make them feel accepted (Burns, 1978). In alignment with the current study purpose, the framework of transformational leadership provided substantial insights into moral and ethical concerns associated with the Nigerian leadership. For example, there were reports of repeated upsurges in bribery, misappropriation of funds, extortion, and self- embellishment among affluent and powerful Nigerians in corridors of power (Ezimma, 2010). The country has suffered a migration to foreign countries, an extremely skilled manpower made up of talented professionals who were saddened by insufficient economic rewards, and unfavorable work condition (Ojo, Ugochukwu, & Obinna, 2011). A transformational approach could motivate the citizens with trust, respect, and loyalty toward their leaders (Bass & Avolio, 1990). The framework of the transformational approach characterize the leader- follower relationship under specific traits that guided the study's conceptual framework (Bass, 1990; Bass & Avolio, 1990);

1. Idealized influence indicates the ability to uphold relevant ideals.
2. Inspirational motivation signifies the passion to motivate followers.
3. Individualized consideration entails tutoring and development.
4. Intellectual stimulation emphasizes goal-accomplishment, creativity, and problem-solving.

Technicalities in transactional leadership also provided substantial theoretical framework for this study. The concept of transactional leadership process is based on leader-follower exchange. The leader provides necessary resources and contingent rewards to followers in exchange for motivation, organizational loyalty, productivity, and effective task execution (Bass & Avolio, 1990). In politics, these activities could translate into a provision of lucrative jobs, subsidies, contracts in exchange for support of desired legislation, campaign contributions, and reelection need (Yukl, 2006). There are three behavioral styles of transactional leadership, namely;

1. Contingent Reward (CR): Guaranteed rewards for qualified followers.
2. Active Management by Exception (AMBE): Reliance on enforcement of rules to mitigate errors
3. Passive Management by Exception (PMBE): Reliance on contingent penalties as corrective measures (Bass, 1985; Bass & Avolio, 1990).

Definition of Terms

The definition of terms and concepts provided below include terminologies used throughout the study to facilitate the understanding of materials presented. These terms are words and expressions commonly used in theories of leadership and organizational development, or those common to the government.

Authority: "Authority involves the rights, prerogatives, obligations, and duties associated with particular positions in an organization or social system" (Yukl, 2010, p. 146). The authority of leaders entails the right to make concrete decisions for the organization.

Collaboration: "If you have a team-based strategy, the values and, specifically, the norms of the organization must emphasize collaboration, consensus, and communication," (Parker, 2008, p. 181). Effective alliances in organizations entail the collective involvement of each person's knowledge and obligation to enhance services and production.

Commitment: Commitment is usually a significant competence in undertaking complex, or difficult tasks. As a result, individuals reach consensus in executing specific decisions or requests effectively (Parker, 2008).

Communication: Through open communication, an organization can enhance innovation by expediting, planning, goal-setting, exchange of information, and reduction of misunderstandings. Communication as an essential leadership skill entails listening, understanding, sympathizing, coaching, and mentoring subordinates to inspire organizational change (Shane, 2009).

Coup d'état: Military regimes often begin with a coup whereby the constitutional powers are confiscated to create an avenue for governance by decrees (Campbell, 2009). This unlawful removal is usually carried out by the army or a group opposed to a prevalent leadership.

Empowerment: The concept of empowerment in the team process entails self-sufficiency, shared responsibility, and encouragement in making significant decisions. The possible advantages validated by research on participative, supportive, and transformational leadership include the notion that justice and neutrality can positively influence the opinions of subordinates when handling procedural justice, and their trust, loyalty, and commitment to the organization (Yukl, 2010).

Ethical Culture: Since Organizational culture is shaped by people, ethics, and structure (Jones, 2010; Yukl, 2010), one of the most significant machineries of governance is making it a priority that leaders follow principled guidelines for their decision-making approaches. This allows for clarity about what is right or wrong (Scott, 2007).

Leadership: Whereas definitions of leadership may vary, the fundamental assertion would be a situation "Whereby intentional influence is exerted by one person over other persons to guide, structure, and facilitate activities and relationships in a group or organization" (Yukl, 2010).

Organization Structure: The process coordinates jobs into larger units, and evaluates the communication process and power structure relations among participants and appropriate entities (Scott, 2007). This structure binds employees together in a formal system of assignment and reporting interactions that controls, organizes, and inspires them to accomplish specific objectives (Gallos, 2006).

Organizational Culture: Since culture is defined as fundamental standards, philosophies, and expectations shared members with an organization (Scott, 2007), it may be impracticable to achieve effective leadership without the controlling force of a culture that provides specific values for essential parameters for improvement of communal trust and obligation (McAuley, 2007).

Power: The power concept indicates how people in the organization influence one another. In the context of leadership, it is the capacity to manage subordinates (Yukl, 2010).

Political System: In the decision-making processes, leaders tactically organize strategies to manage or allocate political power. Appropriate apportionment will integrate the interests of all stakeholders who need to accept the decisions if they are to be implemented (Tichy & Devanna, 1990).

Participative Leadership: A participative leader involves the team in the decision-making process because most members prefer a participative style, even when the decision model requires an autocratic style (Thompson, 2008). Consequently, effective application of participative leadership leads to a better quality of decision-making, acceptance of a decision by participants, satisfaction with the process, and more improvement in decision-making skills (Yukl, 2010).

Resistance/Change Resistance: Applying new measures or technologies and overcoming resistance to change are primarily human resources management issues (Bansal, 2009; Yukl, 2010). The term resistance describes an outcome in which an individual is opposed to the proposal, so leaders must be prepared to deal with possible barriers. This is because structural change comes with deep resentment among subordinates when a tradition has been broken (Yukl, 2010).

Transactional Theory: The transactional Leadership model as explained by Burns (1978), depends on a give-and-take approach which could be "economic or political or psychological in nature" (p. 101. para 2). A transactional leadership style does not favor individualized resources, but sets standards that may create unprecedented pressure from followers, thus, members who are rewarded for meeting expected objectives (Yukl, 2010).

Transformational Theory: Transformational leaders inspire relationships with followers under specific factors, "Idealized influence, inspirational motivation, intellectual motivation, intellectual stimulation, and individualized consideration," (Bass & Avolio, 1990, p. 204). The process occurs where both leaders and the led elevate themselves to upper levels of inspiration and decency (Burns, 1978).

Assumptions

To expressively accomplish any exploration of qualitative research method, attention must be accorded to the underlying assumptions that guide the use of a particular research method (Moustakas, 1994). To explore the understanding of how political, cultural, social and economic conditions in Nigeria influence the lives of Nigerian citizens the following fundamental assumptions were considered;

1. The participants would represent specific geopolitical zones in Nigeria as they stated.
2. The participants would be thorough and sincere in sharing their experiences and feelings about Nigeria.
3. This researcher would assume that expectations contained in the research questions were consistent with the subjects and strategies generated by content analysis of the literature.
4. This researcher would assume that the sampling of data related to the citizens' experience of the leadership system in Nigeria might provide substantial information to illustrate Nigeria's leadership process and complexities.
5. This researcher would assume that analyzing data on its sample population would be representative of all the people of Nigeria (Moustakas, 1994).

Scope

The importance of the scope of the current study process is to establish relevant boundaries (Simon, 2006). In research study, the scope defines the relevant boundaries of the process in determining what would be included and what would be excluded (Maxwell, 1996). The scope of the current study focused on the feelings and experiences of Nigerian citizens living through a leadership process. Whereas all components of management in organizational leadership was taken into consideration, specific focus was on leadership behaviors, skills, and practices in the Nigeria's governmental system. A sample of 12 Nigerian citizens was selected from visiting Nigerians citizens who attended monthly meetings of Org. A and Org. B respectively. Both groups are structurally diverse with visiting Nigerians from different geopolitical regions.

The study relied exclusively on extensive semi-unstructured interviews to gather relevant data. Open-ended and exploratory questions were posed to each study participant in a flexible set-up that allowed them to give accounts individually in their words (Moustakas, 1994). Notes taken during the interview session with individual participants were systematically transcribed and entered into Nvivo 10® software for processing and data coding. Final data input were systematically analyzed through the modified van Kaam data analysis method by Moustakas (1994). Study participant consented to the interview process. The interviews only proceeded when consent forms were signed and received. The study explored how political, cultural, social, and economic conditions in Nigeria influence the lives of Nigerian citizens through lived experiences of two citizens from each of the six geopolitical regions of the country. The study did not include Nigerian citizens in the diaspora, citizens currently in government or direct descendants of past and present Nigerian leaders.

Limitations

Research examiners use limitations to detect potential study weaknesses (Simon, 2006). Qualitative research process may be challenged when objective hypothesis testing procedures are not used: therefore, researchers must consider the goals and limitations of a study in order to appreciate the nature of the research process (Moustakas, 1994). The first limitation included the honesty of participants and threat of inadequate data. The present of researcher, which is often mandatory in qualitative research, can affect the participants' responses. Possible concerns about honesty of participants were mitigated through the confidentiality practices of the study process. The process of Informed Consent explained in details in Chapter 3 encouraged each of the participant to narrate their experiences in the most precise manner without fear of breach of confidentiality. Another limitation is that the study analysis and interpretation would have been time-consuming based on the voluminous nature of data in the qualitative process. To mitigate this shortfall and inspire process swiftness and accuracy, the current study used Nvivo 10® software to systematically code a large file of interview transcriptions.

Delimitations

Delimitations are boundaries established by the research examiner to narrow the scope of the study (Simon, 2006). The current study was delimited by excluding Nigerian citizens in the diaspora, citizens currently in government or direct descendants of past and present Nigerian leaders. The study captured the lived experiences of Nigerian citizens now living under the leadership system. Therefore, Nigerian citizens not currently living in the country were not the appropriate samples. Furthermore, citizens currently in government, or direct descendants of past and present Nigerian leaders were excluded to mitigate possible respondent biases. The demographic component of this study was also limited to geopolitical regions; therefore, issues of tribes, gender, and religions were entirely excluded as they bear no relevance to the study purpose.

Summary

The purpose of the qualitative phenomenological research study was to understand how political, cultural, social, and economic conditions in Nigeria influence the lives of Nigerian citizens through lived experiences of two citizens from each of the six geopolitical regions of the country namely, North-Central, North-Eastern, North-Western, South-Eastern, South-South, and South-Western regions. Chapter 1 presented a synopsis of the study's content, narrated the general problem, and explained the specific problem statements. Using the purpose statement, the chapter established the justification for the study, its consequences in Nigeria's governance processes, and significance in the study of leadership. Chapter 2 presented an in-depth literature review on Nigeria, the history, leadership, and the dynamics of the governance process. The chapter will also review literatures on research methods and relevant leadership theories.

Chapter 2
Literature Review

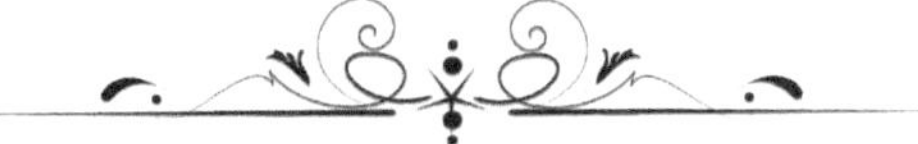

As Cooper (1988) suggested, a review process must emphasize study relevance, purpose, coverage, organization, and audience. The literature review in the current study focused on process applicability by prioritizing research findings, methods, theories, and applications.

The purpose of the qualitative phenomenological research study is to understand how political, cultural, social and economic conditions in Nigeria influence the lives of Nigerian citizens through lived experiences of two citizens from each of the six geopolitical regions of the country namely, North-Central, North-Eastern, North-Western, South-Eastern, South-

South, and South-Western regions. The general problem addressed is that the quality of life that the Nigerian citizens experience is dependent on the leadership and when the leadership if flawed, the citizens may suffer (Abdullahi, Yahya, & Yelwa, 2012). The specific problem studied is that the Nigerian leadership is flawed and exacerbates the political, economic, cultural and social problems which directly influence the way its citizens' experience living. Chapter 1 presented a synopsis of the study's content which included a narrative of the general and specific problems; problem and the purpose statements, and the significance of the study in the field of management in organizational leadership. Vast discussions about relevant theories which directed the research findings were also presented with discussions on the evaluation of fundamental expectations, scope, limitations, and delimitations of the study.

Chapter 2 presents the literature review relevant to the study problem statement and primary research question. The literature review investigates and synthesizes materials in such legible manner to systematically support the research study (Cone & Foster, 2006). The content covers a broad examination of relevant texts that guided the study in five areas:

1. Works that offered insight into past and present leadership processes in Nigeria;
2. Literature that defined and discussed political, economic, cultural, and social development, as well as the process and dynamics of leadership;
3. Literature that represented organizational design, development, and practice;
4. Literature that consisted all aspects or components of the research process;

5. Literature that included all methods and process of qualitative phenomenological research study.

A literature review is a demonstration of the examiner's understanding of the proposed study (Moustakas, 1994). The process can help identify with recommendation, the necessity for further research (Gall, Borg, & Gall, 1996). The literature review plays a significant role in (a) delineating the research problem, (b) searching new areas of inquiry, and (c) gaining insights into methods and techniques (Gall, Borg, & Gall, 1996; Hart, 1998). As Cooper (1988) suggested, a review process must emphasize study relevance, purpose, coverage, organization, and audience. The literature review in the current study focused on process applicability by prioritizing research findings, methods, theories, and applications.

The current study was conducted through a qualitative phenomenological research study. Qualitative design examines lived experiences of an individual participant allowing them to give a description of their lived experience in a natural environment (Moustakas, 1994). Phenomenological researchers aim at describing the experiences research participants have in common as they live through a phenomenon (Kvale, 1996). The review of relevant literature sets the constructive framework that helped to answer the research question: How do Nigerian citizens describe their experience of living under economic, political, cultural, and social hardships? The study was accomplished with the existential-phenomenological methodology. Existential phenomenological researchers focus more on participant's experiences and actions, rather than conformity or behavior (Moustakas, 1994).

The research design was performed through semi-structured interviews of 12 Nigerians, two citizens from each of the six geopolitical regions of the country. In the process, participants were asked to describe their experiences of living under a system marred by economic, political, cultural, and social issues. The researcher developed a combined description of the essential aspects of the phenomenon as experienced by all of the participants, focusing on "what" they experienced and "how" they experienced it (Moustakas, 1994). The theoretical framework for this study integrated essential theories of modern leadership for contextualizing the experiences of Nigerian citizens who were living in unstable governance conditions. Data were collected through a face-to-face interview with each study participant. Relevant themes were identified from the interview data analysis and was used to process the research findings.

Researcher in the current study focused on the research goal by identifying central issues, reconciling conflicts and generalizing results. The study used a qualitative approach to reveal the nature of definite conditions as experienced by people who were living through it (Moustakas, 1994). The research examiner derived a new understanding from the occurrence, built different theories and academic perspectives on the matter, and realized existing complexities within the phenomenon (Moustakas, 1994). The review revealed a gap in the literature relating to the application of leadership practices in Nigeria from its independence in 1960 to the present. Major part of the review showed inconsistencies in the Nigeria's leadership structure as it pertains to political, cultural, social and economic conditions of the citizens (Achebe, 1983; Polgreen, 2007). Disclosures from finding highlighted the significance of the theories of leadership as they correlate three essential elements: the leaders, the followers, and the surrounding situation and context. Furthermore, Contingency Leadership theory (Stogdill, 1995), Transactional, and Transformational Leadership theories (Burns, 1978; Bass, 1985; Tichy & Devanna, 1986) were adequately reviewed.

In the present-day society, the demand for effective leadership based on hope, aspiration, and performance standards have increased (Yukl, 2013). To meet these challenges, leaders must be equipped with transformational individualities, including personality values, confidence, expertise, influence tactic, and relevant behaviors (Stogdill, 1995). The dynamics of management in organizational leadership were revealed in the review as they corroborate the problem statement. For example, Ezimma (2010) substantiated reports of repeated upsurges in bribery, misappropriation of funds, extortion and self- embellishment among affluent and influential Nigerian leaders. Polgreen (2007) noted a catastrophic mix of fraud and ignorance among leaders in undermining the electoral structure. One of the most significant machineries of governance, prioritized in contemporary management is the emphasis and insistence that leaders follow ethical guidelines in their policymaking (Premeaux, 2009). The literature review explored the relevance of the ethical system of leadership. Ethical decisions are directed by individual morals and values. Ethics are those doctrines that guide personality such as compassion, morality, devotion, objectivity, honor, and respect for others, consistency with keeping promises, and quest of distinction, (Stogdill, 1995; Yukl, 2010).

Title Search

The term "leadership" bear a connection to the research purpose and was applied in the search process. This method revealed vast resources in leadership from various sources. SAGE Knowledge was used to review major journals relating to community, culture, politics, and social development. SAGE Knowledge provided a reliable collection of full-text journals covering several topics that addressed the study goals. Multiple databases from the University of Phoenix Library were also used. These included EBSChost, Emerald, ProQuest, Gale PowerSearch, ProQuest Dissertations, and Theses. Others such as Google Scholar, Best-In-Class, Benchmarking Reports, and Sage assisted the study examiner in locating additional relevant literatures.

Relevant keywords were used in various combinations to find the most accurate and pertinent information related to the research topic and purpose as shown in Table 1. The search enabled a review of 130 journals and peer reviewed articles

Table 1

Breakdown of Literature Reviewed

No.	Key Word Search	Journals	Books	Peer-reviewed Articles	Web/ Others	Total
1.	Leadership	20	5	10	5	40
2.	Nigerian History	20	1	15	5	41
3.	Nigerian Government	15	1	10	10	36
4.	Transformational Leadership	20	1	25	5	55
5.	Transactional Leadership	15	1	20	5	45
6.	Contingency Leadership	10	1	10	1	26
7.	Research Methods	10	5	10	2	26
8.	Qualitative Research	10	3	15	2	30
9.	Phenomenological Research	10	1	15	2	28
Total		130	19	130	37	327

respectively, 19 books, and 37 other sources including computer-generated libraries and internet links. Key words that were used when conducting research for the study titled, "A phenomenological study of the influence of Nigerian leadership on the life of its citizens" are Nigeria, government, leadership, culture, community, politics, military, embezzlement, corruption, social, political, economic, cultural, elections, development, tribes, collaboration, transformation, transactional, organization, development, and performance. Others are qualitative, quantitative, phenomenology, and existential.

The Nigerian Government websites and specific databases were used to retrieve relevant information about remarkable terms which includes: Nigeria's organizational culture, Nigeria's geopolitical culture, The Nigerian Constitution, Nigeria's leadership timeline, Nigeria's political history, sectarian violence in Nigeria, Nigeria's electoral process, economic hardship, and economic development. Terms related to the leadership concepts and theories in the proposed study are: leadership failures, leadership effectiveness, socioeconomic and political issues, leadership ethics, organizational development, organizational design, leadership models, leadership theories, trait model, leadership theories, transformational theory, transactional theory, laissez-faire, and dynamics of leadership models, organizational paradigms, and management philosophy. Terms related to research methodology included: case study, phenomenological, grounded theory, ethnographic, qualitative and quantitative, realistic phenomenology, constitutive phenomenology, existential phenomenology, hermeneutical phenomenology, transcendental phenomenology, existential phenomenology, constitutive phenomenology, realistic phenomenology, Heidegger, Husserl, types of phenomenology, and phenomenological research guidelines. Several topics and terms were excluded from the proposed research process because they bear no relevance to the subject matter. They are; race, chieftaincy titles, biological, gender, and affirmative action.

Historical Outline: Early Leadership Theory

The ancient Greek conception of management or leadership was characterized by heroic virtues. Machiavelli's approach challenged leaders to be firm, calm, and inspire the zeal for upholding the authority, power, and order in government (Bass, 1995). A more contemporary and scientific approach to leadership developed overtime under three general eras: "the trait era, the behavior era, and the contingency era" (Navahandi, 1995, p. 37). The trait era relied on individual features to assess personalities; behavior approach prioritized tasks to examine conducts in which leaders engage, whereas the contingency era focuses on the scale of situational control (Yukl (2010).

Trait Model. One of the earliest leadership models occurred in the Trait Era of the Late 1800s to Mid-1940s. The era was dominated by the notion that leaders are born rather than made. The process evaluated individual characteristics to identify significant traits (Navahandi, 1995). Measurement based on individual traits assessed "dominance, social sensitivity, moodiness, masculinity, and physical appearance," (Chemers, 1995, p. 84). However, studies of more than forty years provided little evidence of substantiality and proved otherwise (Navahandi, 1995). Thus, variation and ambiguities in findings corroborated the fact that traits only do not classify leadership," (Chemers, 1995, p. 84).

Behavior Model. A failure of the Trait Model was mainly due to the premise that traits such as loyalty, integrity, and honesty could not be measured adequately, whereas behaviors could be observed and measured objectively (Yukl (2010). Lack of results triggered a so-called Behavior Era which continued until the 1970s (Navahandi, 1995). Measurement of the behavior approach prioritized tasks rather than qualities with rating scales, interviews, and other systematic assessments, identifying specific behaviors in which leaders engage (Yukl (2010).

Contingency Model. The measurements of leadership effectiveness remain inconclusive as the study of behavioral patterns failed to address significant organizational issues related to group productivity and member satisfaction. However, the Contingency Era that advanced from the 1960s to the present provided more clarity in predicting leadership effectiveness. In fact, personality, style, or behavior of effective leaders are reliant on the situation in which they find themselves (Navahandi, 2006). Measurement in the contingency approach is based on a scale of situational control developed by Fred Fielder under three features: leader-member relationships, task arrangement, and position power (Chemers, 2006). The reliability of the contingency approach soon diminished by a heated debate over methodology and concept interpretation. Researchers questioned the "situational variables and general predictive validity" (Chemers, 1995).

Contemporary Theory

Dynamics of a search and advancement of leadership effectiveness changed with the emergence of more contemporary models. Two foremost theories namely Transformational and Transactional theories emerged. Transformational model opposes the notion that leadership resides in a person, but focuses on empowering of all levels of individuals to assume leadership roles (Bass, 1990; Bass & Avolio, 1990). In a contrast, transactional Leadership model as explained by (Burns, 1978) dwell on a give-and-take approach in engaging labor. Transformational and Transactional theories are explained in details:

Transformational Theory. The approach opposes the notion that leadership is innate and focuses on the empowerment at all levels of individuals to assume leadership roles. Transforming leadership, wrote Burns (1978), "occurs when one or more persons engage each other in such a way that leaders and followers raise one another to higher levels of motivation and morality," (p. 101). Technicalities of transformational leadership model played a crucial role in analyzing this study's findings. According to Yukl (2010), transformational leaders characterize relationships with followers under specific factors, "idealized influence, inspirational motivation, intellectual motivation, intellectual stimulation, and individualized consideration" (p. 276). Leaders who exert "idealized influence" and "inspirational motivation" project a required future, set parameters, and determine performance level. Followers subscribe to such a philosophy without restriction to their growth. "Intellectual motivation" is manifested when leaders express innovation and help followers to become creative. Leaders who exert "individualized consideration" assist with task-related issues, including work, stress, and social environment (Yukl, 2010).

Transactional Theory. The transactional leadership model falls short of creating morale or stimulating creativity, but prioritizes exchange of labor for wages through an economic, political or psychologically inspired give-and-take approach. The approach motivates a form of leadership effectiveness based on legitimate power and respect for rules and traditions (Burns, 1978). Transactional leadership style does not favor individualized resources, but sets standards that create unprecedented pressure from followers; thus, followers are rewarded for meeting expected objectives. There are three behavioral styles of transactional leadership, namely; Contingent Reward (CR) and Active Management by Exception (AMBE), and Passive Management by Exception (PMBE) (Bass, 1985; Bass & Avolio, 1990).

Leaders in the CR process provide followers with guaranteed rewards when followers fulfill their assumed responsibilities. An effective leader in the transactional setting would accomplish tasks by setting practical objectives, communicate comprehensively, allow followers to independently manage their tasks, and encourage them with motivation and specified rewards (Bass & Avolio, 1990). In the PMBE setting, leaders rely on contingent penalties and relevant corrective measures in managing recognizable lapses or deviations in performance values. Leaders in the AMBE process identify mistakes and rely on enforcement of rules to mitigate errors (Bass & Avolio, 1990).

Nigeria: Historical Background

Nigeria gained its independence from Great Britain on October 1, 1960 (History, 2011). From a constitutional structure of a parliamentary form of government, it was restructured into a federation of three major regions; North, West, and East. These regions retain a significant degree of constitutional autonomy, whereas the federal government reserves exclusive powers in national security, external relations, commercial, and monetary policies. Nigeria became a federal republic in October 1963 when it drafted a new constitution and created a fourth region called Midwest (History, 2011).

Since this independence and the declaration of a republic, Nigeria has been ruled by seven military officers and seven civilians, witnessing more than eight coups with three leading to the assassination of the leaders. As shown in Table 2, the country has also endured consistent switching of governments from constitutional models to military leaderships (History, 2011). A civil war erupted in 1967 over constitutional revision and leadership uncertainty and ended in 1970, leaving the country with 12 states structured under strict military rule. The military governor of the eastern region, Lt. Col. Emeka Ojukwu had declared the independence of the constituency as the "Republic of Biafra" in May 1967 resulting in the hostile and bloody civil war that ended in 1970 with the defeat of Biafra (History, 2011; Nigeria, 2011; Uche, Falola, Heaton, & Matthew, 2009). Numerous political events that had besieged this country between 1900 and 1959 were sufficient signs that the country would face problematic governance. A major concerns on the list of these challenges would be how to surmount issues of nationalistic and task-oriented leadership (Odion & Omolere, 2011). Today, Nigeria is democratically governed; however, it has gone from 12 to 36 current states and the federal capital region called Abuja as shown in Figure 1. These 36 states were regrouped from three regions into six geopolitical zones in order to simplify governance and to assign greater autonomy to ethnic minority groups. A timeline of geographical and zonal division in Nigeria since the independence in 1960 are as follows,

1. 1960-1963: Three Regions
2. 1963-1967: Four Regions
3. 1967-1976: 12 States
4. 1976-1987: 19 State
5. 1987-1991: 21 States
6. 1991-1996; 30 States and Capital
7. 1996-2014: 36 States and Capital (History, 2011; Suberu, 1994).

Figure 1

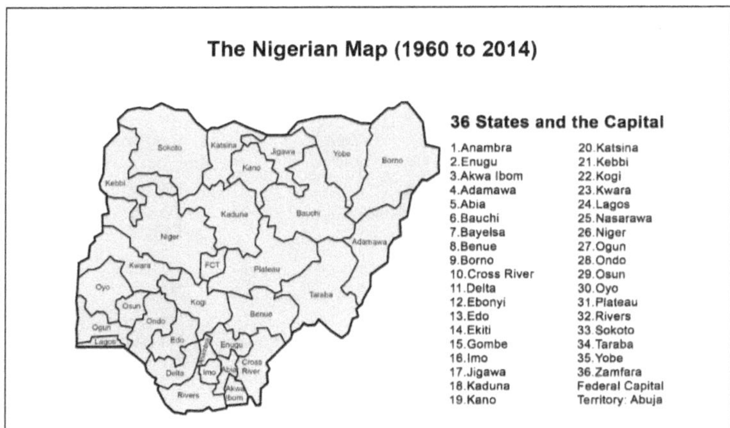

Figure 1. Nigerian current map showing 36 states and a capital, Abuja.

Note. From the researcher, as cited in (History, 2011; Suberu, 1994)

Table 2

Taxonomy of Nigerian Leadership from 1960 to 2014

Name of Leader	Tenure	Period	Leadership Position	Leadership Type	Exit Process
Alhaji Abubakar Tafawa Balewa	October 1, 1960 – January 15,1966	6 Years	Prime Minister	Elected	Coup/ Assassination
General Thomas Aguiyi-Ironsi	January 15, 1966 – July 29,1966	6 Months	Military Leader	Coup	Coup/ Assassination
General Yakubu Gowon	July 29, 1966 – July 29, 1975	9 Years	Military Leader	Coup	Bloodless Coup
General Murtala Mohammed	July 29, 1975– February13, 1976	I Year	Military Leader	Coup	Coup / Assassination
General Olusegun Obasanjo	February 13, 1976–October1, 1979	3 Years	Military Leader	Coup	Civilian Handover
Alhadji Shehu Shagari	Oct 1, 1979-Dec 31,1983	4 Years	Executive President	Elected	Coup
Major-General Muhammadu Buhari	December 31, 1983 August 27, 1985	2 Years	Military Leader	Coup	Coup
Major- General Ibrahim Babangida	August 27, 1985 – August 27,1993	8 Years	Military Leader	Coup	Resignation
Chief Ernest Shonekan	August 27, 1993 – November 17, 1993	3 Months	Interim President	Appointed	Resignation
General Sani Abacha	November17, 1993 – June 8,1998	5 Years	Military Leader	Coup	Died in Office
General Abdulsalami Abubakar	June 8, 1998 – February 23, 1999	1 Year	Military Leader	Appointed	Civilian Handover
Gen Olusegun Obasanjo	May 29, 1999 – May 2007	8 Years	Executive President	Elected	Civilian Handover
Alhaji Umaru Musa Yar'Adua	29 May 2007 – 5 May 2010	3 Years	Executive President	Elected	Died in Office
Goodluck Ebele Jonathan	6 May 2010 until Date	4 Years	Executive President	Elected	Currently in Office

Note. Timeline of a political process subjecting Nigeria into a tenure of seven military dictators and seven civilians leaders, as cited in History (2011); Nigeria (2011), Government and Political Conditions (2011).

History of Leadership in Nigeria: A Summary

The purpose of the qualitative phenomenological research study was to understand how political, cultural, social and economic conditions in Nigeria influence the lives of Nigerian citizens through lived experiences of two citizens from each of the six geopolitical regions of the country. The general problem addressed in the study was that the quality of life that the citizens of the country experience is dependent on the leadership and when the leadership is flawed, the citizens may suffer (Abdullahi, Yahya, & Yelwa, 2012). Issues with political leadership in Nigeria started since her independence in 1960 (Rice, 1998). A philosophical question about post-colonial Nigerian history was posted:

"Now that Nigeria had gained its independence, the question that dogged the country was: what is the country going to do with it? As many Nigerians have observed, it was easier to gain freedom than to exercise it" (Udogu, 2009, p. 125).

Nigeria's first experience with leadership came after gaining independence in 1960 from Great Britain. Alhaji Abubakar Tafawa Balewa was elected the Country's first prime minister 1957, and kept this office when the federation became independent in 1960 (Nigeria Unshackled, 1960). Alhaji Balewa's leadership faced numerous challenges in a governmental structure that was new at the time. The federal government constitutionally controlled national security, external relations, and commercial and monetary policies, leaving the regions (Northern, Western, and Eastern) with substantial amount of sovereignty (History, 2011). The weakness of Alhaji Balewa's regime left the country with political uncertainties, ranging from sectionalism to tribal-based conflicts. For example, Ogunbadejo (1979) stated that leadership values, critical matters, and public interests were frequently subordinated to sectional necessities in particular situations. The sectional divide between the leadership and the masses was noticeable, leaving a greater part of the country practically excluded from involvement in the economic and socio-political processes (Ogunbadejo, 1979).

Alhaji Balewa's experiment with leadership was short-lived: In 1966, he was assassinated in an aborted bloody coup by some young army officers led by one Major Chukwuma Kaduna Nzeogwu. This dark moment began military involvement in Nigeria's political history. Army General Thomas Aguiyi- Ironsi took over power on Jan 15, 1966, suspended the Constitution, and promulgated several decrees that characterized his leadership. Coupled with the inability to draft a constitution that would satisfy the interests of all segments of the country, Aguiyi-Ironsi's regimet was to resolve the ethnic tensions at the time, but the crisis worsened (History, 2011).

After six months of ineffective governance experiences, General Aguiyi-Ironsi was assassinated in another coup (History, 2008). General Yakubu Gowon assumed power on July 29, 1966 and led the country into a civil war that lasted from 1967 to 1970. However, on July 29, 1975, he was also removed from office through a bloodless coup. The period of 1960-1970 saw "instability and civil war;" the darkest moment of Nigerian history, as inconsistencies with leadership and organizational structures created severe socio-political crises that cost the nation millions of lives (Udogu, 2009; History, 2011; Nigeria, 2011; People, 2011; Profile, 2011). Brigadier (later General) Murtala Muhammad established himself as a Nigerian leader through a coup on July 29, 1975, and ousted General Gowon while the latter was out on an official visit in Kampala, Uganda. In 1976, General Muhammad was assassinated in another attempted coup, and second in command Brigadier Olusegun Obasanjo (later Lt. General) was quickly selected to replace him as the head of state (History, 2008). Leadership of this country during this period became a turn-by-turn affair on the part of a plethora of army officers (History, 2008).

The second republic came to reality when General Obasanjo led a transition from military rule to democracy, handing over leadership to Alhaji Shehu Shagari on Oct 1, 1979. In furtherance of the army culture, the government led by Shagari was removed from office in another coup, thus bringing Nigeria's second republic to a sudden halt. Another round of the military regimes in Nigeria resumed after this coup. Major General Muhammadu Buhari was declared the Head of State with total command over the country's governance along with a council of military officers in his cabinet. However, Buhari did not last too long in office (History, 2008).

General Ibrahim Badamasi Babangida, his Chief of Staff, took power in August 1985 through a bloodless coup, alleging uncontrolled human rights abuses (History, 2008). In prolongation of the coup tradition, General Babangida's second-in-command, General Sani Abacha seized power on Nov17, 1993 from Chief Ernest Shonekan, whom General Babangida had installed to head an interim government. Abacha died in June 1998 at the presidential villa in Abuja, upon which his successor, General Abdusalami Abubakar swiftly announced a transition to democracy that signaled the end of Nigeria's military era (History, 2008).

Nigeria's journey to the third republic started with a reemergence of the retired General Obasanjo on May 29, 1999, through an electoral process. After a constitutionally allowed two-term tenure that lasted for eight years, Alhaji Umaru Musa Yar'Adua took over the mantle on May 29, 2007 through another election, but died in office from liver complications. The vice president, Goodluck Ebele Jonathan assumed power on May 6, 2010 to complete late Yar'Adua's tenure. In 2011, President Jonathan ended that tenure and ran successfully for another term that has kept him in office until this date, as Nigeria's president (History, 2011). An illustrative taxonomy of Nigerian leaders is shown in Figure 2 with visual images identifying Nigeria's past leaders and their tenures as they progressed from 1960 to 2014 (History, 2008).

Figure 2

Taxonomy of Nigerian Leaders (1960 to 2014)

Figure 2. A flowchart identifying Nigeria's past military and civilian leaders as they progressed over the years.

Note. From the researcher, as cited in History (2008, 2011); Nigeria (2011); Profile (2011).

Current Findings: Nigeria's Leadership Dynamics.

The purpose of the qualitative phenomenological research study was to understand how political, cultural, social and economic conditions in Nigeria influence the lives of Nigerian citizens through lived experiences of two citizens from each of the six geopolitical regions of the country namely. Literature review included current findings about the dynamics of Nigeria's leadership process as it corroborates its prevailing political, cultural, social and economic conditions. Nigeria is endowed with a wide variety of natural resources that underscore its potential for a vibrant economy. These resources are used by households and industries scattered across the regions (Nigeria, 2013). Unfortunately, leaders were slow to develop these minerals compared to the scope of deposits available (Madueke, 2008; Udogu, 2009; History, 2011). Studies have attributed this underdevelopment to government instability, economic setbacks, and inefficient leadership intensified by corruption and political instability (Madueke, 2008).

The theory of politics, economics, culture, and social structure of governance are intertwined. Studies by Koenig and de Guchteneire (2007) on political governance of cultural diversity focus on the challenge of democracies, suggesting the zeal to design policies that respect cultural diversity. Such policies must prioritize collective participation and foster the shared bonds and a sense of solidarity that strengthens the workings of a democratic society (Madueke, 2008). The purpose of the qualitative phenomenological research study was to understand how political, cultural, social and economic conditions in Nigeria influence the lives of Nigerian citizens through lived experiences of two citizens from each of the six geopolitical regions of the country. Reviewing relevant literatures on the leadership systems that exacerbate the circumstances dovetails the problem statement discussed in Chapter 1.

James MacGregor Burns attributes political leadership to personal drive, communal inspiration, governmental drive, profession skills, and career ambitions (Pospisil et al., 2004). Political studies highlight not only leadership opportunities, but also effective leadership tools and the ability to apply those (Pospisil et al., 2004). The absurdity of Nigeria's political flaws was that each region and the entire populace existed under various oligarchs who syphoned the national wealth and paid little or no attention to the ordinary person's predicament (History, 2008; Abdullahi, Yahya, & Yelwa, 2012). In fostering the literature review of this study, it was relevant to develop a clear understanding of the theories of politics, economics, culture, the social idiosyncrasies, and how they factor into Nigeria's leadership dynamics.

Political Factors. The term 'politics' originated from the early Greek word 'polis', meaning "city-state." Then, the term was distinctively used for the civic community in ancient Greece. A clearer explanation was provided by Machiavelli, Pospisil, Churchill, and von Heyking (2004). Consequently, noted Pospisil et al., the world is also separated into states, systematically structured according to variables that include ethnicity, race, gender, religion, and political principles. Niccolo Machiavelli's definition of politics emphasizes power influence and the circulation of goods within the community (Pospisil et al., 2004). Plato (1988, 650b) defines politics as the skill of caring for the soul – ascribing the role of governmental leadership in encouraging the quality or ethical distinction between individuals. Plato's analysis attributed power or wealth as a sign of bad leadership (Pospisil et al., 2004).

There is no doubt that political issues in Nigeria were troubled over an unstable leadership process (Madueke, 2008). The purpose of the qualitative phenomenological research study was to understand how political, cultural, social and economic conditions in Nigeria influence the lives of Nigerian citizens. Literature review revealed that the root of Nigeria's political instability started immediately after independence in 1960. Since this period, political leaders twisted the process to prolong their tenures, whereas elected officials transformed the public treasury into a personal gold reserve (Madueke, 2008). In the current study, participants specifically focused on their experience as Nigerians living in Nigeria, in economic, political, cultural, and social hardships, while they reflected on various leadership anguishes they have lived through. Singh (2011) attributed Nigeria's detours on the way to democracy as an authoritarian political system operated without a defined guiding ideology. Furthermore, the leaders oppressed the masses, silenced any opposition with hired thugs, influenced census numbers to favor their cohorts and party affiliates, and fraudulently manipulated elections with reckless abandon (Ogunbadejo, 1979).

Pospisil et al.'s (2004) explanations are a clear indication that politics and leadership go hand-in-hand. Their discussion clearly indicates a vivid impression that an effective application of political theories depends not only on the caliber of leadership, but also on surrounding elements. Consequently, in Nigeria, a major challenge to democratic governance lies in both the leadership selection process and the entire electoral process. Olu-Adeyemi (2012) argued that the electoral processes were perverted; political parties dominated by corrupt influences, including godfathers and ex-military leaders, and elections often discriminatory, non-participatory, and unconstitutional. As a result, the leadership circle was corrupt and loyal to godfathers and patrons. This dysfunctional political process had subjected Nigeria into a tenure of seven military dictators and seven civilian leaders, and exposed the system to eight coups with three leading to assassinations (History, 2011). Furthermore, Nigeria had consistently switched between constitutional and military models of governments, each incurring a tremendous amount of lethal conflicts and ongoing regional disputes (History, 2011).

Economic Factors. Economics and politics are deeply related to issues of political leadership and economic development. Both concepts are intertwined in the philosophy of any nation's political and social history (Economy, 2009). The term economics is very broad. According to Göçme (2008), it originated from the ancient Greek words 'oikos' (house) and 'nomos' (law). However, issues of modernity gave rise to the concept of political economy as an independent discipline. From another perspective, economy as a multidimensional concept refers to a system of capital accumulation involving actors competing for power and hegemony concerning resources management (Göçme, 2008).

Literatures corroborated dynamics of political leadership, and economic development (Economy, 2009) with issues of Nigeria's resources management. As a result, citizens living in the system were left with varieties of experiences that were explored in the current research study (Agbiboa, 2012). No modern nation or state enjoys an autonomous economy: if one were to fail, it would cause a domino effect, collapsing or disabling other systems (Economy, 2009). Thus, despite Nigeria's oil prosperity and its rank as the world's eighth largest oil producer, the masses remain impoverished (Agbiboa, 2012). A 2006 report by the United Nations Human Development Index summarized Nigeria's economic shortfalls with alarming figures. The Index ranked Nigeria 159 out of 177 states: roughly 70% of Nigeria's residents make a living from incomes less than $1 a day, and life expectancy has declined to an unacceptable 47 years (Agbiboa, 2012). Today, Nigeria cannot favorably compete with its counterparts' development evolvement, especially in the areas of quality of life, infrastructure, fundamental needs of life, and technology. This problem was traced to inadequate and unqualified personnel, lack of proper funding, and technical resources to drive the vehicle of development immediately after independence (Lawal et al., 2012).

Cultural Factors: Halloran's (2007) definition of culture emphasizes particular values, tools, and practices shared by a population with a collective social identity. A correlation of culture and leadership style can affect performance and determine leadership effectiveness (Shah, Iqbal, Razaq, Yameen, Sabir, & Khan, 2011). The complexity of culture and organizational leadership pose inescapable challenges in management because differences exist among individuals, populations, countries, and organizations. There are concerns about how democracy can be maintained through a reconciliation of cultural diversity with the social construction of trust and solidarity necessary for the preservation of an independent polity (Koenig & de Guchteneire, 2007). Culture is the vehicle that drives leaders' actions (Shah, et al., 2011). Literature review showed that Nigerian leaders have attempted to superimpose behaviors and traits on the masses from their own religious or ethnic societies (Kuhlke, 2006). This practice left the citizens wholly disconnected with the system. The current qualitative phenomenological research study investigated the above mentioned cultural anomalies by exploring the research question on how Nigerian citizens described their experience of living in economic, political, cultural, and social hardships.

Another issue centers on integrating minority groups into the national citizenry with equal rights. Guchteneire (2007) believed that constitutional arrangements could serve as a mediation tool between or among different groups, their shared privileges of independence, and a citizen's rights to participate in the governance process. These points underscored the prevailing cultural issues faced in Nigeria's leadership processes. Under a similar perception that culture drives behavior, a study by Tsai (2011) ties behaviors to satisfaction. Tsai (2011) argues that the followers' satisfaction can be achieved by adjusting leadership behavior to meet the established organizational mission and values. Organizational culture, leadership behavior, and satisfaction are interconnected. Culture and politics are related and indicate the aspect of people's values that concerns their knowledge and practice of politics (Fasan, 2002).

Literatures review shows that Nigeria is enriched with about 250 ethnic groups with different languages, beliefs, and religions (History, 2008). The three key ethnic communities are the Hausa and Fulani tribes in the north, Yoruba tribe in the southwest, and the Igbo tribe in the southeast. The Northerners are predominantly Muslims whereas the Southerners are mostly Christians (History, 2008). While some studies found richness in Nigeria's multilayered diversity, others see this as detrimental to its socio-political progress. In the Nigeria's system, ethnic diversity has been accompanied by ethnic prejudices; hence mistrust, religious extremism, and social conflicts (Tajudeen & Adebayo, 2013).

The complexities of managing this democracy have created smoldering grievances between various regions, ethnic groups, and religions with millions of casualties. For example, Muslim-dominated states have denied their Christian residents their privilege to enact policies suiting their religious values, thus undermining Nigerian statehood (CultureGrams, 2013). There are contradictions in the application of democracy throughout Nigeria's multicultural population. The complications, argued Tajudeen and Adebayo, (2013) may explain why the nation has been threatened by North and South dichotomy, sectarian violence, and a complex governance culture and structure.

A different dimension of studies on culture and leadership comes with Geert Hofstede's cross-cultural comparative study that suggests building familiarity with the cultural resemblances, and differences between and among leaders (Munley, Couto, & O'Neill, 2010). The dimensions explained as follows are, "power distance, uncertainty avoidance, individualism, masculinity, and long-term orientation" (Moskowitz, 2009, p. 3);

1. Power Distance Index (PDI): Under this index, the measurement of how the underprivileged members of the society and the less powerful entities recognize the fairness of power distribution becomes a necessity.

2. Individualism (IDV): Individualism and collectivism are two opposing concepts denoting the range of integrating individuals into groups. Individualistic aspect of the index seeks cultures where ties between persons are loose, whereas collectivism refers to cultures where people are integrated from birth into solid, organized in groups, especially extended families.

3. Masculinity (MAS): The index of masculinity and femininity discusses gender complexities and management. The measure of roles between genders is fundamental in organizational management.

4. Uncertainty Avoidance Index (UAI): Measuring the acceptance of uncertainty and ambiguity specifies how members of organizations are culturally programmed to express their feelings in unstructured circumstances.

5. Long-Term Orientation (LTO): This index addresses long-term versus short-term orientation and stresses prospect, frugality, and perseverance. Organizations that embrace long-term orientation prioritize future issues and nurture realistic standards. They are concerned with rewards and the ability to adapt. Short term learning cultures prioritize values of the past and present and are concerned with balance, custom, image, and accomplishment of social commitments (Moskowitz, 2009; Minkov & Hofstede, 2011).

Social Context. From a political and economic framework, literature review revealed possibilities, challenges, and relevant approaches to social growth associated with Nigeria's governance (Rubin & Sherraden, 2005). Although most leaders would seek avenues to alleviate unfavorable economic conditions, citizens still may face many challenges, including poverty, illness, premature and preventable mortality, and hunger (Tajudeen & Adebayo, 2013). Studies by Grais, Gerstl, Guthmann, Djibo, Nargaye, and Guerin (2007) identified inadmissibly high mortality ascribed to measles spread throughout some West African countries, including Nigeria. This occurred despite the mitigation strategies introduced by a comprehensive initiative of the World Health Organization (WHO) and United Nations Children's Fund (UNICEF). The Economist Intelligence Unit (2012), quoting The National Bureau of Statistics, revealed that a high number of Nigerians exist in sheer penury and can barely afford the necessities of food, shelter, and clothing. Thus, the poverty level soared to 69% in 2010, compared with a 54% rate in 2004. Chukwuemeka and Ntunde (2011), in a report on eradicating hunger in Nigeria, revealed how leadership lapses through corruption, injustice, and a lack of development structure could cause social insufficiency and crippled any quest for poverty alleviation. The aforementioned statistics justified the relevance of the study purpose, seeking to understand how political, cultural, social, and economic conditions in Nigeria influence the lives of Nigerian citizens through lived experiences of two citizens from each of the six geopolitical regions of the country.

Social development entails an all-inclusive model that encompasses managing the well-being of the people, community, and the society (Miah, 2008). In Nigeria, the leaders are insensitive to the troubles of ordinary people, causing a trickle-down effect on the populace in rural and urban centers (Niworu, 2013). This concern has generated an environment that draws communal conflicts and undermines national security. The failure of government to address lacks in the social system left the entire country in a sociopolitical chaos, whereby citizens provided their water, health services, and electrical power generators (Niworu, 2013).

Leadership in Nigeria: A SWOT Analysis

Organizations use a SWOT (Strengths, Weaknesses, Opportunities, and Threats) analysis as a starting point for developing a strategic plan, including goals and objectives (Foster, 2011). The SWOT analysis in this study served as a tool to investigate leadership problems in Nigeria as they influenced citizens. The purpose of the qualitative phenomenological research study was to understand how political, cultural, social and economic conditions in Nigeria influence the lives of Nigerian citizens through lived experiences of two citizens from each of the six geopolitical regions of the country. Conducting an SWOT analysis offered an in-depth focus on areas that needed consideration and also provided avenues for an efficient action plan (Beagrie, 2004). An SWOT investigation of Nigeria's governance background inquired into leadership performances and underperformances, and enriched the study findings with practical approaches to providing a better management (Valentin, 2001).

Strengths. SWOT Analysis (2010) identified three major strengths related to Nigeria's economic stability. The first is that the nation's endowment with a large population indicates an abundant supply of cheap (albeit unskilled) labor and a growing consumer market (SWOT Analysis, 2010). Second, taxation is comparatively low with a paltry 5%, corporate tax 30%, and individual income tax rising progressively to a top rate of 25%. Last, the country's oil reserves remain the second highest, and natural gas reserves are the highest, in Africa (SWOT Analysis, 2010).

Weaknesses. Nigeria is plunged by political uncertainties ranging from sectionalism to religious fanaticism, tribal-based oppositions, and fatal conflicts (Ogunbadejo, Oye (1979). Leadership development has been decelerated by tenure inconsistency and has resulted to more than eight coups, assassination of three leaders, and a three-year civil war (History, 2011). As a major weakness, failure of government to address shortages in the social system has left the entire country in a sociopolitical chaos and the masses without amenities, including water, health services, and light (Niworu, 2013).

Opportunities. Prevalence of large oil reserves can continue as the country's principal economic driver (SWOT Analysis, 2010) and create more economic possibilities. Enriched with about 250 ethnic groups with different languages, beliefs, and religion, Nigeria's diversity is viewed by some as an asset (History, 2008) in forging a more robust and united nation. There are also opportunities in reducing corruption in the public sector. SWOT Analysis (2010) revealed some improvement in reducing corruption, and with a pro-market government, this should continue to improve.

Threats. Nigeria's multicultural nature, especially regarding Christian and Muslims religions, continue to be a source of tension (SWOT Analysis, 2010). Another threat stems from the election process. According to Odion and Omolere (2011), the process has been hijacked by individuals who have organized themselves into a cabal with the ultimate purpose of determining the pace of political choices and structures in their regions. Last, the cumulative incidents of corruption and violence threaten Nigeria's quest for good governance and have thus become issues of public concern (Idris, 2013).

Ethical System. Ethics establishes rules and unwritten laws to govern behaviors (Yukl, 2010). Individual morals direct ethical decisions and values are those doctrines that guide personality. These include compassion, morality, devotion, objectivity, honor and respect for others, consistency with keeping promises, and quest of distinction, (Yukl, 2010). A review of ethics might play a significant role in the current study. For instance, in the problem statement discussed in Chapter 1, Lawal, et al. (2012) state that since achieving independence in 1960, Nigeria has only produced the caliber of leaders enthralled by corruption and governmental wrangling.

Adherence to ethical guidelines in making policies is one of the most significant machineries of governance prioritized in contemporary management (Yukl, 2010; Jones, 2010). Ezimma (2010) documented notorious corruption cases in Nigeria that have undoubtedly hampered the practice of ethics in every segment of the government. Integrity is a value that cannot be compromised in leadership because, in tandem with an unwavering commitment to purpose, it is necessary to effective leadership (Cuilla, 1998; Avolio & Gardner, 2005). Without a commitment to fundamental values that direct the organization, the managing structure can deteriorate rapidly (Azuka, 2009).

Ethics entail the practice of the principles of right and wrong, and evaluate the moral standards of an individual, a culture or group (Waskey, 2008; Preissle, 2008; Jones, 2010). The knowledge of the foundation of ethical reasoning can positively affect the decision-making process (Premeaux, 2009; Bateman & Snell, 2007). The mechanics of an ethical system are based on Moral Philosophy, Universalism, and the Caux Principles. Moral Philosophy is the application of rules and values in making decisions about what is right or wrong. Ethics scholars identify Universalism as a primary ethical system that requires preservation of specific values that organizations need to function. The Caux Principles are global support for principled capitalism and a partnership in order to instill a fair, free, and transparent global society (Bateman & Snell, 2007). These archetypes of the ethical structure are systematically explained:

1. Moral Philosophy: The application of Moral Philosophy in the management structure is an inevitable task for a leader who would inspire trust and transparency in the governance process. Bateman and Snell (2007) describe Moral Philosophy as rules, and values, used in making decisions about what is right or wrong in the constituency.

2. Universalism: Ethics scholars identify Universalism as a primary ethical system that requires individuals to adhere to specific exemplary standards that would add value to the functioning of a society (Bateman–Snell, 2007). Most descriptions of the mechanisms of management and compatible theories about effective leadership focus on specific behaviors used to influence followers (Yukl, 2006).

3. Caux Principles: The Caux Round Table (CRT) is a global advocacy group for promoting honorable capitalism and collective collaboration to instill a rational, open and transparent society. This set of ethical principles was devised by transnational business administrators based in Caux, Switzerland, in partnership with corporate leaders from major countries, including Japan, United Kingdom, and the United States (Bateman & Snell, 2007).

Relativism. In an organization where different cultures exist, managing ethics may take a different dimension. Literature review generated several journal articles and studies associating Nigeria's governance instability with lapses in ethical standards. As noted earlier, Nigeria has witnessed since independence in 1960, the caliber of leaders enthralled by corruption (Lawal, et al., 2012). Ethics establishes rules and unwritten laws to govern behaviors. Relativism is an ethical behavior structured on how others behave. Leaders transmit ethical influence both down and across large organizations (Schaubroeck, et al., 2012). Relativism articulates ethical conduct and recognizes the existence of different ethical viewpoints (Bateman & Snell, 2007).

Egoism and Utilitarianism. Egoism is a behavioral pattern that maximizes benefits for a particular individual. The concept inspires the greatest good for oneself under the perception that the well-being of society increases as so long everyone follows this system (Bateman & Snell, 2007; Waskey, 2008; Preissle, 2008; Jones, 2010). While the application of moral thinking advocates "doing the right thing," Egoism promotes the greatest good for oneself. On the hand, Utilitarianism focuses on the ideal that moral worth of any action must result in the greater good of a larger number of people than it may harm (Bateman & Snell, 2007; Jones, 2010).

Virtue Ethics. Virtue ethics emphasizes the role of one's character and the qualities that it represents. Organizations sometimes go beyond conventional rules and require an individual to display only good behavior. Whereas an organization's rules provide ethical guidelines, persons can go beyond rules by applying their virtues such as belief, decency, and truth. Aristotle's exploration of morality highlights judgment, virtue, and character as three significant elements of human decency. Thus, individuals remain the primary referent of the study of ethics and morality (DeGeorge, 2010). Virtue ethics reveals the ideals in a person; identifies the admirable qualities that form ethical demeanor, and helps others to acquire these values (Johnson, 2009). Moral laws, social standards, business structures, and moral people are all interconnected in shaping societal moral uprightness. According to DeGeorge (2010), when structures and laws are immoral, people are encouraged to act immorally, and vice versa. Therefore, moral people and moral structures reinforce each other because moral people are needed to create and sustain moral structures. Virtue theorists prioritize moral character in discussions of ethics, emphasizing conscientiousness, compassion, and responsibility rather than a traditional reliance on rules and government regulations (Craig, 2002).

Organizational Development. The OD concept involves challenging choices about distribution of power, obligation, and accountability into units; it entails a coordination of responsibilities and motivation of the people who accomplish them; it maximizes an organization's capability to generate value (Jones, 2004). The purpose of the current study is to understand how political, cultural, social, and economic conditions in Nigeria influence the lives of Nigerian citizens through lived experiences of the citizens from each of the six geopolitical regions of the country. The mechanics of Organizational Development (OD) played a significant role to understand the influence of Nigerian leadership on the quality of life of its citizens. The OD functions are more than just tools and techniques; they radiate fundamental principles that require participation, learning, justice, and equality. The OD process also inspires effective communication, and information process, mutual obligation, and other factors that would engage people and foster strategic means to solve a problem (Gallos, 2006). Literature review shows that OD and management policies in Nigeria have worsened in what some scholars classified as 'the management theory jungle' (Redding, 1994; Koontz, 1980).

Organizational Design and Decision-Making Processes. The process of organizational design coordinates people, information, and technology, and balances them with organizational purpose, vision, and strategy (Autry, 1996). Organizations rely on the framework of organization design to make choices on operational structure. The policies provide essential tools for leaders to acquaint themselves in order to manage decisions and behaviors effectively in their organizations (Galbraith, 2002). Organizations are operated by people who make decisions: A leader plans, organizes, and controls the decision process. The effectiveness and quality of those decisions determine how fruitful and efficient the project will be (Jones, 2010). According to Huber (1986), the appropriateness of the decision-making standard determines the organization's success. A review of relevant literatures regarding efficient decision-making processes offered significant insight into the leadership challenges faced by the Nigeria's structure. George (2012) stressed that issues of public policy and decision-making process in Nigeria are subjected to values associated with a veneration for tradition, paternalism, hero, and age grade.

Organizational Culture: Culture is defined as the fundamental standards, philosophies, and expectations shared by members of the organization (Scott & Davis, 2007). It may be difficult to achieve effective leadership without the controlling force of an organizational culture. Leadership provides organizational values as essential parameters for improving communal trust and obligation (McAuley et al., 2007). Organizations, therefore, could prioritize membership loyalty, enlist collective involvement, and coordinate various sectors to solve integrative problems (Scott & Davis, 2007). Review revealed religion as an essential sociocultural influence of management practices in Nigeria (George, 2012). This influence is consistent with conflicts over ethnic and religious differences believed to have threatened Nigeria's existence as a sovereign entity (Mercy, 2012). For an organization to attain an active culture that is compatible with its structural components, the leader could create an organizational framework that inspires hard work and cultivates the right attitudes. (Shane, 2009; Jones, 2004).

Organizational Structure: Organizational structure binds employees together in a formal system of assignment and reporting interactions that controls, organizes, and inspires them to accomplish specific objectives. The particular problem in the current study was that the Nigerian leadership is flawed and exacerbated the political, economic, cultural, and social problems which directly influence the way citizens experience living (Abdullahi, Yahya, & Yelwa, 2012). The structure of organization in governance has significant implications in the study findings. The process of organizational structure coordinates jobs into larger units and evaluates the communication process and power structure relations between participants and appropriate entities. An informal structure uses various incentives to motivate employees with the least supervision in a situation that jeopardizes effective power sharing and goal management. Power is a dependent variable in governance and may change as a result of uncertainty, substitutability, and its centrality to the organization (Scott & Davis 2007).

Historical Outline: Research Method

The current study adopted the phenomenological study as a method to explore an understanding of how political, cultural, social and economic conditions in Nigeria influence the lives of Nigerian citizens currently living through the experience. Phenomenological study investigates human understanding influenced by the perception that individual and experience are an effective source of knowledge (Moustakas, 1994; Dreyfus & Wrathall, 2006; Martino, 2010). Under this segment, this paper presents the historical development of a phenomenological study. Knowledge and experience conveyed the appropriate foundation that inspired the growth of phenomenology. The roots are traced back to Plato's philosophy of Platonic Idealism associated further back with the Hindu and Buddhist beliefs (Tymieniecka, 2002). The term "phenomenology" originated from the Greek word "phenomenon," meaning "appearance," To some conflicting extents, the early development of the concept was accredited to other philosophical engagements. These are: René Descartes and the model of the methodological skepticism; British Empiricism associated with Locke, Hume, Berkeley, and Mill, and Immanuel Kant's Idealism (Moustakas, 1994; Kruger, 1988; Krupp, 2010; Tymieniecka, 2002).

Today, however, the study of Phenomenology is primarily ascribed to the vision of Edmund Husserl, provoked in his 1901 project, "Logical Investigations" (Husserl, 1965). Husserl's first development came with his Classical Phenomenology, focusing on "descriptive psychology" and later as a transcendental and eidetic knowledge of consciousness. Martin Heidegger, however; challenged this notion by introducing personal understanding and experience of being and the being itself, and focused on metaphysical ontology rather than Husserl's foundational discipline (Adams & Manen, 2008; Porter, 1998). In the first half of the 20th century, the diversity in the traditional phenomenology inspired broad categories of phenomenology namely; Realistic Phenomenology, Transcendental Phenomenology, Hermeneutic Phenomenology, and Existential Phenomenology. The categories explained as follows are distinguished by specific features;

Realistic Phenomenology: Realistic phenomenology associated with Husserl's early formulation thrived in Germany in the 1920s. The concept explores the collective principles of several matters such as individual actions, purposes, and personalities (Moustakas, 1994; Kruger, 1988; Adams & Manen, 2008). Under this construct, the philosophy of law to the study of phenomenology was introduced by Adolf Reinach; philosophy of ethics, religion, and anthropology was initiated by Max Scheler; philosophy of the human sciences was initiated by Edith Stein, whereas aesthetics, architecture, music, literature, and film were established by Roman Ingarden (Moran, 2000).

Transcendental Phenomenology: True knowledge could be derived from personal involvement (Moran, 2000). Philosopher, Edmund Husserl advocated Transcendental Phenomenology as a concept interpreted correctly to capture events through descriptions of personal experience (Moustakas, 1994; Kruger, 1988; Sokoloski, 1999). Husserl believed that phenomenology is a human science deep-rooted in application because it explores the source of knowledge and explains the assumptions and groundwork of human understanding. (Adams & Manen, 2008; Moran, 2000; Porter, 1998). Basic themes of transcendental phenomenology are "intentionality," "eidetic reduction," and "constitution of meaning." These themes describe thinking, feeling, and acting process about the things, and the surrounding environment. Transcendental depicts the nature of eidetic reduction that characterizes the phenomena. Eidetic phases of a specific phenomenon are often explained by imaginative variations (Moustakas, 1994; Kruger, 1988; Porter, 1998). As a phenomenology of consciousness, intentional analysis is always constitutive as it explains how the meanings of things are consciously constituted (Moustakas, 1994; Kruger, 1988; Sokoloski, 1999). Transcendental reduction withdraws the researcher from the natural attitude whereas the constitution of meaning portrays a return from consciousness (Moustakas, 1994; Kruger, 1988 ;).

Hermeneutic Phenomenology: Hermeneutical phenomenology explores the interpretive aspects of human experience, the understanding and engagement of the individuals and the environment (Moustakas, 1994; Kruger, 1988; Adams & Manen, 2008). Unlike the descriptive approach that characterizes the transcendental phenomenology, the process is said to be hermeneutical because it can be interpretive (Moustakas, 1994; Kruger, 1988; Seamon, 2010). Human consciousness is revelatory, thus Heidegger, who championed this concept believed that description and interpretation work hand-in-hand (Seamon, 2010). The primary themes of hermeneutic phenomenology are "interpretation," "textual meaning," "dialog," "preunderstanding," and "tradition" (Tymieniecka, 2002).

Existential Phenomenology: Existential phenomenology exceeds conventionality or behavior, but focuses on personal experiences and actions of the individual (Moustakas, 1994; Kruger, 1988). The current study relied on existential phenomenological method to adequately capture participant's experiences and actions. Existential phenomenology is so named because it explores the human existence and experience relating to individual values, purpose, emotions, and choice or action in tangible circumstances (Moustakas, 1994; Kruger, 1988; Adams & Manen, 2008; Moran, 2000; Porter, 1998). The Basic themes of existential phenomenology are “lived experience,” “modes of being,” “ontology,” and “life world” (Tymieniecka, 2002). In the existential approach, a person is not just subjected to the influences of the environment, but also possesses inner understandings, and can comparatively interpret the events of the moment as relates to the interactions with the social world.

Conclusion

The current literature review identified the gap between leadership and the influence of Nigerian leaders in the quality of life of the population. The lack of effective leadership in Nigeria created extraordinary social problems unbearable to the citizens. The purpose of the qualitative phenomenological research study was to understand how political, cultural, social, and economic conditions in Nigeria influence the lives of Nigerian citizens through lived experiences of two citizens. The general problem addressed in the study was that the quality of life that the citizens of the country experience is dependent on the leadership and when the leadership is flawed, the citizens may suffer (Abdullahi, Yahya, & Yelwa, 2012). This study was necessary because Nigeria is one of those countries endowed with enough natural and valuable resources to boost its economic and sociopolitical management, yet citizens suffer from economic deprivation (Lawal, Imokhuede, & Johnson, 2012).

Chapter 2 explained the literature review of the proposed study – incorporating a broad examination of relevant texts that guided the study process. The review revealed historical texts associated with related concepts of the study's theoretical framework. These include books on leadership ethics (Cuilla, 1998; Avolio & Gardner, 2005), research ethics (Sales & Folkman, 2000), leadership (Bass & Avolio; Bass, 1990; Burns, 1978; Vroom & Yetton, 1973; Stogdill, 1948; Fiedler, 2006; Chemers, 1997), research methods (Moustakas, 1994; Van Manen, 1990; Seidman, 1991; Patton, 2002; Schatzman & Strauss, 1973). Most existing information about Nigeria's historical and leadership dynamics were also reviewed. These includes scholarly journals and articles (Rice,

1998; Achebe, 2003; Kehinde, 2009; Polgreen, 2007; 2009; Agbiboa, 2010; Ezimma, 2010; Odion & Omolere, 2011; Joseph, 2012; Lawal, Imokhuede, & Johnson, 2012; Abdullahi, Yahya, & Yelwa, 2012; Idris, 2013).

The current study added to the body of literature in leadership because a closer look at the influence of the Nigerian leadership on the quality of life of its citizens was substantially presented. Whereas some of the literature searches were not relevant to the current study, Chapter 2 comprised a comprehensive investigation of relevant texts that offered insight into past and present leadership processes in Nigeria; literature that discusses political, economic, cultural, and social development in Nigeria; the process and dynamics of leadership; and technicalities of organizational design, development, and practice. Chapter 3 describes the design procedure and methodology that directed the proposed study.

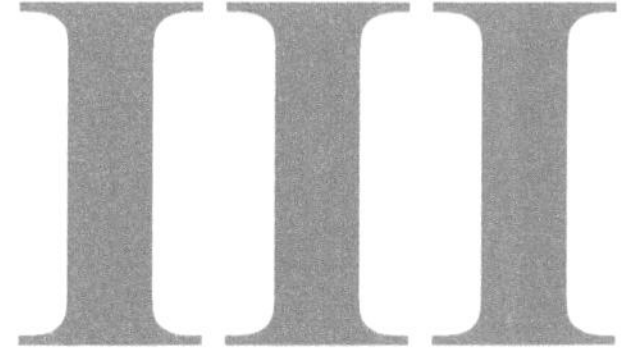

Chapter 3
Methodology

■ The study scratched underneath the phenomena and provided detailed descriptions that reflected citizens' experience in their own accounts (Maxwell, 2005). The interpersonal connection built into the phenomenological process (Van Manen, 1990) could not have been achieved through the counting of figures, classification of geometric features, or construction of statistical models.

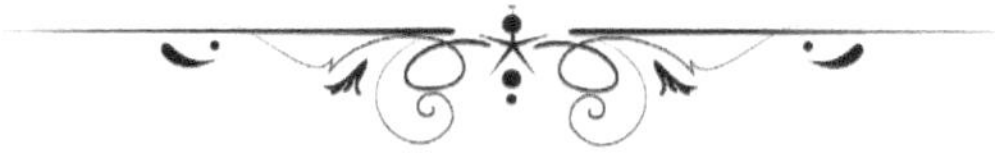

Chapter 2 examined relevant literature about the history of Nigeria, its leadership, and the dynamics of the governance process. The section also included the historical context of the research approach. The purpose of the qualitative phenomenological research study was to understand how political, cultural, social and economic conditions in Nigeria influence the lives of Nigerian citizens through lived experiences of two citizens from each of the six geopolitical regions of the country namely, North-Central, North-Eastern, North-Western, South-Eastern, South-South, and South-Western regions. The Nigerian leadership has been flawed and exacerbated the political, economic, cultural, and social problems which directly influence the way its citizens experience living in Nigeria. This explains the need to conduct a qualitative phenomenological study.

Chapter 3 describes the responsibility of the researcher, as well as the research methodology, population, instrumentation, data collection process, and the development of data analysis. Other elements in the chapter encompass the study population, the sampling of participants, informed consent and confidentiality, internal and external validity, and reliability. The section also used the process of research methodology and design to answer the following research question: How do Nigerian citizens describe their experience of living under economic, political, cultural, and social hardships?

Method and Design

The qualitative phenomenological research design was conducted to explore the influence of Nigerian leadership on the quality of life of its citizens. The current study was necessary because of insufficient existing literature pertaining to how political, cultural, social, and economic conditions in Nigeria influence the lives of Nigerian citizens living in the system. The study explored individual in-depth experiences of 12 Nigerian citizens; two from each of the six geopolitical regions of the country. Nigeria currently made up of 36 states are grouped into six geopolitical zones in order to simplify governance and to assign greater autonomy to ethnic minority groups (History, 2011). Drawing samples from each of the geopolitical zones increases the validity of the study in ensuring that findings are an accurate representation of the phenomena. Participants were drawn from citizens who visited the United States for the monthly meetings of Org. A and Org. B respectively. This segment of the study proposal also provided justification for the selection of qualitative phenomenological approach as a method.

A qualitative study was appropriate for this study because the process involved an in-depth exploration of the phenomenon for people who were experiencing the issues (Patton, 1990). Phenomenological method was selected to examine people's observations, comprehension, and perspectives on a specific circumstance (Moustakas 1994). Existential phenomenological methodology was appropriate because the study satisfactorily captured participant's experiences and actions rather than dwelled on conventionality or behavior (Moustakas, 1994). Under this setting, the quantitative approach, which is processed by testing theories, measuring numbers, and analyzing statistical methods (Jencik, 2011) would have entailed trying to place a square peg in a round hole. Besides, the ideals of quantitative research focus on the arithmetic of variability, where researchers redefine concepts by applying the mechanics of variable in a process incompatible with qualitative designs (Black, 1999). The Mixed Research method was not considered for this study because a combination of testing and generation of hypothesis or theories were not relevant. The Mixed Research approach combines quantitative and qualitative data in a single study and generates a final report through a mixture of statistics and qualitative data (Babbie, 2001). These qualities are incompatible with the rudimentary purpose of this study.

Phenomenology refers to individual's perception and understanding of situations or events. The current study answered questions relating to people's experience (Moustakas 1994; Flood, 2010; Orbe, 2009; Adams & Manen, 2008; Hammersley, 2004; Hamilton, 2005; Mapp, 2008; Willis, 2007). The study examined people's observations, comprehension, and perspectives on a particular circumstance (Moustakas 1994; Christensen & Turner, 2010). Phenomenological researchers rely exclusively on extensive interviews, using open-ended and exploratory questions in a format that allow participants to describe their experiences and perceptions in their words (Moustakas, 1994). Phenomenological researchers also collect data by encouraging participants to share and discuss their experiences. The researcher develops a combined description of the essential aspects of the phenomenon as experienced by individual participants, and the way they are experienced (Moustakas, 1994).

An applicable sample size for a qualitative study should satisfactorily provide answers to the research question. A distinctive sample size is from five to twenty-five interviewees with direct experience of the research subject (Moustakas, 1994). Participants in the current study served as the major data source. To align with typical procedure, in-depth interviews were conducted on two citizens from each of the six Nigerian geopolitical regions. The study then adopted an approach suggested by Moustakas (1994) that the interview process must establish and construct the interviewee's experience in such that the composition reflects the meaning.

Appropriateness of Design

In a qualitative study process, the researcher aims at understanding the world from the participant's perspective with emphasis on how and where the events occur (Moustakas, 1994). The researcher defines in descriptive form, the meaning and understanding of the phenomenon that usually encompasses an in-depth investigation of the problem from participants experiencing it (Moustakas, 1994). The current study started with general research enquiries and involved an extensive amount of information on a smaller population processed into a form that offered consistency and used verbal descriptions to portray situations related to the subject (Moustakas (1994). A qualitative study was suitable for this process because the approach besides other features, focused on people and situations in real environments (Maxwell, 2005). The researcher derived a new understanding, built different theories and academic perspectives on the matter, and realized existing complexities within the phenomenon (Moustakas, 1994). The qualitative method is more universal and evolving, with a defined emphasis, appropriate strategy, efficient measurement tools (e.g., interviews), and efficient analyses that develop and possibly change (Patton, 2002). Phenomenology is compatible with qualitative research because in the process, individual observations define engagements and responses. As Cohen, Kahn, and Steeves (2000) noted, individuals understand engagements based on how they were perceived. Thus, phenomenological method remained suitable because the process examines people's observations, comprehension, and perspectives on circumstance under investigation (Moustakas 1994).

There might have been a few reasons why the phenomenological method would have been unfit for this study. Critics argue that 'subjectivity,' 'description,' and 'interpretation' associated with the phenomenological approach impel a lack of scientific vigor that may threatens process validity (Van Manen, 1990). Another reproach arises from a lack of practicality attributed to researcher's suspension of presuppositions about the study phenomenon (Sartre, 1958). However, the descriptive strategies of the current phenomenological approach namely; intuiting, bracketing, analyzing, and describing mitigated any possible threats of process validity (Kvale, 1983). Intuition enabled sheer openness to the meaning ascribed to the phenomenon experienced by the participants. Bracketing enabled a suspension of assumptions and presuppositions that drove the study rigor. Analyzing corroborated relevant data to identify the essence of the phenomenon, described distinctively and critically communicated the study finding (Kvale, 1983).

There were other significant grounds why phenomenological design was appropriate for the current study. The standard of shared experience synonymous with phenomenology connects the research question and objective. The purpose of the current qualitative phenomenological research study was to understand how political, cultural, social and economic conditions in Nigeria influence the lives of Nigerian citizens. The study centered on the citizens living through a governmental system. A phenomenological approach enabled the researcher to unravel the complexities of this purpose (Moustakas, 1994). The study scratched underneath the phenomena and provided detailed descriptions that reflected citizens' experience in their own accounts (Maxwell, 2005). The interpersonal connection built into the phenomenological process (Van Manen, 1990) could not have been achieved through the counting of figures, classification of geometric features, or construction of statistical models. By aiming to recount events through a strategic exploration of feelings of the participants who have experienced the phenomenon, existential approach became appropriate.

As explained by Pollio, Henley and Thompson (1997), existential phenomenology incorporates two philosophies, one focusing on specific perception of human existence, and the other possessing relevant methods of exploring that existence. The existential phenomenologist focuses squarely on issues that individuals experience in their daily lives (van Manen, 1990). Existential phenomenology was appropriate for this study because the method engaged participants to objectively narrate their feelings about the phenomenon. Through this process, the researcher gained an essential understanding as well as provide a rich and detailed description about the lived condition of each study participant (Moustakas, 1994). Hence, achieving these details would have been inevitable if the study relied on quick survey handouts and arithmetical calculations (von Eckartsberg, 1998).

The study used existential-phenomenological approach to search for the vital meanings of participants' experiences (Groenewald, 2004). Existential phenomenological method sufficiently captures participant's experiences and actions rather than dwell on conventionality or behavior. The process explored the fundamental correlation between participants' understanding and the phenomena, enabling the researcher to retrieve relevant descriptions of participants' experience, and their understanding of living in the system under study (Patton, 2002; Adams & Manen, 2008). The study adopted the existential phenomenological approach because under this method, a participant is not just subjected to the influences of the environment, but also possesses inner understandings, and can comparatively interpret the phenomena as it relates to the interactions with the social world (Moustakas, 1994).

Qualitative methods such as grounded theory, ethnography, and case study were not used for the current study because of process incompatibility. Each possesses specific attributes that were inappropriate for the purpose of the present phenomenological study. For instance, grounded theory focuses on developing a theory about the process of where existing methods are insufficient. In grounded theory, researchers concentrate on generating theories from data consisting of inductive and deductive thinking, and explain the workings of some aspect of the social world (Strauss & Corbin, 1998). The qualitative ethnography describes the characteristics of a culture through close observations, readings, and interpretations. Ethnographers gain entrance to participants' culture to facilitate necessary observation and interaction to gather data (Miles & Huberman, 1994). The case study research method relies on observations, documents, interviews and other data generated by several sources to examine issues. The case study method uses a particular location and last over a period (Richards and Morse, 2007).

Population

Population describes elements with common characteristic established by the researcher for the sampling criteria (Moustakas, 1994). Prior to the data collection process, the research examiner in the current study identified a population of potential groups, individuals, or organizations that possess collective characteristic defined by the sampling criteria (Moustakas, 1994). The sample for this study were selected based on following criteria;

1. Participants' have experience of the phenomenon under investigation.
2. Participants' willingness to consent to the study process.
3. Participant's willingness to participate in extensive interview process that might involve routine follow-ups.
4. Participants' consent to be recorded during the interview process.
5. Participants' permission regarding the publication of data from the interview (Moustakas, 1994).

The population for the current qualitative phenomenological research study were Nigerians citizens presently residing in Nigeria, West Africa. Participants were recruited from Nigerian citizens who visited the United States for monthly meetings of Org. A and Org. B. Meeting information of both associations are public and were accessed through their respective websites. The groups are tagged Org. A and Org. B to shield the actual names for confidentiality. Org. A is a worldwide professional, non-political, and non-governmental group partnering with Nigerians currently living in Nigeria to promote excellence in human capital development. Org. B is one of the foremost Nigerian non-profit organization, addressing socio-cultural, economic, and public policy needs of members. Both groups are structurally diverse with Nigerians from different geopolitical regions and hosted visiting Nigerian citizens to monthly community meetings. Networking session of the meetings in each group is open to the public.

Recruitment Strategy

Participants for the current study were recruited from Nigerian citizens who visited the United States for monthly meetings of the League of Org. A and Org. B . Both organizations were found from the listing of Nigerian organizations through a Google search. Both organizations held their membership meetings monthly. The leaders were officially informed and requested to announce the study to their members before and during their general meetings. Official requests were also sent to the leaders to use their respective premises for the interview process. All meetings in both groups were open to every Nigerian as well as the public during networking. This enabled the study examiner to gain entrance into the meetings throughout the process. The researcher visited the meeting locations after the requests were granted as shown in Appendix B and initiated the research process. The study examiner interacted with members of respective organization after the meeting periods to discuss the research process. The selection process drew 12 Nigerians, two citizens from each of the six Nigerian geopolitical regions from both organizations. Identification codes were assigned to each selected contact for communication purposes during the research process.

Sampling

Sampling refers to drawing elements, such as people and objects from a population for analysis. The standard goal of sampling is to obtain a representation that is similar to the population. A perfectly representative sample would be a "mirror image" of the population from which it is selected (Moustakas, 1994). Purposive sampling method was used in the proposed study. Purposive sampling focuses on specific characteristics of the population of interest and enable the research examiner to answer the research questions (Manen, 1997) appropriately. The ultimate quality of the qualitative research study may be dependent on the selection of samples (Moustakas, 1994; Schatzman & Strauss, 1973). The selection process stated Schatzman and Strauss (1973), is a practical obligation shaped by availability of time, interests, target participants, and hosts.

Challenges in finding appropriate sample for research study was thoroughly evaluated in the current research study. Kvale (1996) stated that variations in qualitative methodologies can affect the concept of data saturation in qualitative study. In other words, noted Seidman (1991), samples in some studies might be limited by availability of individuals to conveniently participate. The phenomenon therefore detects both the method and the kind of participants (Hycner, 1999). The concept of data saturation adopted by the current study set a limit for capacity of the needed data (Kvale, 1996; Seidman, 2006). The study examiner interacted and recruited participants continually until the appropriate sample size was reached. An applicable sample size for a qualitative study provides satisfactory answers to the research question. A typical sample size is from 5 to 25 interviewees with direct experience in the study area (Moustakas, 1994).

The study examiner selected purposive sampling because it is considered the most effective non probability approach to identifying the primary participants (Welman & Kruger, 1999; Moustakas, 1994). Purposive Sampling entails a selection of the most productive or information-rich sample to response to the research question (Manen, 1997). The process enables a purposive choice of study participants based on their knowledge about the study phenomenon (Moustakas, 1994). Purposive sampling was appropriate and allowed the researcher to gain complete knowledge about the phenomenon from participants who were currently experiencing it (Manen, 1997; Marshall, 1996; Clifford, 1997; Mapp, 2008). An applicable sample size for a qualitative study would provide satisfactory answers to the research question. A typical sample size is from 5 to 25 interviewees with direct experience in the study area (Moustakas, 1994). To align with this procedure, the sample size of the current study was 12 participants. The study conducted interviews with two citizens from each of the six Nigerian's geopolitical regions categorized as, (a) North-Central, (b) North-Eastern, (c) North-Western, (d) South-Eastern, (e) South-South, and (f) South-Western. Drawing samples from each of the geopolitical zones increases the validity of the study in ensuring that findings are an accurate representation of the phenomena.

Informed Consent

Bailey (1996) cautions study examiners about deceptive practices, suggesting that dishonesty might prevent beneficial insights whereas process uprightness and confidentiality reduces suspicion and encourages trust and sincere responses. This study was cautious in handling two fundamental research validity engagements; Principle of Voluntary Consent and Informed Consent (Moustakas, 1994). Principle of Voluntary Consent is an ethical practice that "people should never participate in research unless they explicitly and freely agree to" (Moustakas, 1994). Informed Consent is a written statement explaining the study process to participants prior to the study. The Institutional Review Board (IRB) of University of

Phoenix played a supervisory role in ensuring that the current study met required standards to protect the rights, privacy and welfare of study participants. Proposal for the current study was submitted to the IRB for review, and was adequately approved before study examiner progressed with collection of samples.

The study was conducted on two citizens from each of the six Nigerian geopolitical regions who currently reside in Nigeria. Each study participant was informed verbally and through consent form about the purpose of the current study. Moustakas (1994) suggested that obtaining permission from research participants is not enough; they must be briefed on the process to enable them make an informed decision. This briefing includes their rights of confidentiality, which would entail protecting their names and other personal information from the study analysis. Among other stipulations, the informed content must include, the right of the participant to (a) participate, (2) decline, or (c) withdraw from the study at any occasion. Participants wishing to withdraw from the study shall inform the researcher through the contact information listed on the informed consent form. Penalty should not be involved in the event of withdrawing from the study (Moustakas).

Prior to the interview, the consent form were handed over in person to each individual who consent to take part in the study. The ink-signed consent forms were collected by the researcher prior to the data-collection process. Moustakas (1994) suggested that data collection can only proceed when consent form is signed and received from each participant. Signing the informed consent means that the participant understands the study purpose, would corporate in the study process, and would be treated with the utmost respect (Moustakas, 1994). Each of the participants in the study received a copy of the signed informed consent form on the scheduled day of the interview. All informed consent forms were signed with inks and locked in a safe deposit box for safekeeping and confidentiality. All information will be retained for three years before they are destroyed. Paper forms will be shredded while the electronic information will be permanently deleted from the system.

The “Informed Consent: Participation 18 Years of Age and Older” form shown in Appendix A was used to secure consent from participants. Appendix B is a sample of signed “Permission to Use Premises” form which enabled the researcher to secure the interview venues to initiate and execute the sample-collection procedure. Participants wishing to withdraw were asked to inform the researcher through the contact information listed in the informed consent form. Such participants would be removed from the list. All paper documents related to such participants would be shredded and electronic files deleted.

Confidentiality

The current Qualitative Phenomenological Study involved human subjects who were engaged exclusively in extensive semi-unstructured interviews (Moustakas, 1994). Research involving human subjects must meet required ethical standard in protecting the rights of the participants. This study did not commence until all protocols including the signing of the consent forms were accomplished. Gaining participant’s permission was not be enough; they were briefed on the process to enable them make informed decisions (Moustakas, 1994).

This study strictly adhered to the following protocol for protecting the rights of human subjects; (a) gaining informed consent from study participants, (b) protecting participants from any harm, (c) protecting the privacy of participants, and (d) adhering to professional ethics (Moustakas, 1994; Yin, 2009).

The current study used investigative questions as contained in a copy of the Interview Questions shown in Appendix D to collect primary data from participants through extensive interviews and other interactions. The interviews were conducted individually at the organization's facility. Participants' names were represented with assigned codes (See Figure 3). Whereas anonymity safeguards participants' identity, Neuman (2006) noted, "confidentiality means that information may have names attached to it, but the researcher holds it in confidence" (p. 139). The concealment of all subjects was assured through the use of secured log-ins, passwords, codes, and folders to identify individual matters. For instance, the research conducted interviews with two citizens from each of the six Nigerian geopolitical regions. As shown in Figure 3, the six geopolitical zones are coded as follows: (1) North-Central: NC-1 and NC-2, (2) North-Eastern: NE-1 and NE-2, (3) North-Western: NW-1 and NW-2, (4) South-Eastern: SE-1 and SE, (5) South-South: SS-1 and SS-2, (6) South-Western: SW-1 and SW-2. The study examiner also used 'Org. A' and 'Org. B' for the two participating groups to protect their identities.

Interviews were recorded, transcribed and saved in the computer server protected with passwords and electronic file-backups. Access to the box required numeric combination known to only the researcher. Original documents and all research data gathered in the interview process would be secured safely in a safe deposit box for a period of three years. Research data included notes taken during the interviews, transcripts, tape recordings, and text messages. After the three-year period, research documents will be shredded while the electronic information will be permanently deleted from the system.

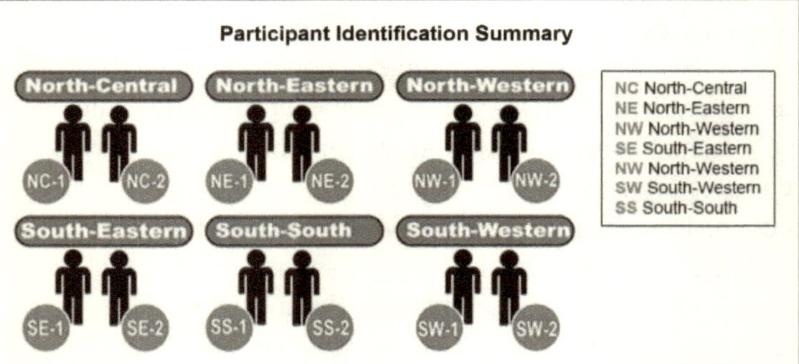

Figure 3. Data-identification summary. Interviews will be conducted on two citizens from each of the six Nigerian geopolitical regions. To protect participants' identity, names and geographical region will be represented with assigned codes.

Note. Created by the researcher as cited in Moustakas (1994).

The Geographic Location

The current study was limited to visiting Nigeria professionals who are members of two diaspora groups; Org. A and Org. B . Both are international professional organizations. Each group held their meetings every month in their respective facilities where they host gatherings and receptions for variety of Nigerians who visit the United States for various reasons. Interviews were conducted with individual participants in the facility of respective organizations.

Data Collection

The current study drew two citizens from each of the six Nigerian's geopolitical regions. The data were obtained through in-depth interviews with selected members of Org. A and Org. B respectively. The major data collection process used by phenomenologists is in-depth interviews (Moustakas, 1994). The outline of actual data collection process that directed this study were particularized in this section. There were four data-related fundamental questions that characterized reliability of the research process (Moustakas, 1994). Thus, the method and process for this research study was brought into clear focus, because the forthrightness of the answers to questions below were established.

1. **Needed data:** Questions about the types of data that were needed helped the researcher to visualize possible sources to create a clear understanding of their treatment.
2. **Data location:** Where this researcher derived the data was fundamental to the design project because data-gathering from obscure or inaccessible areas may complicate the process.

3. **Data gathering:** This process comprised confidentiality agreements, privacy laws, and ethical values. Knowledge of where data was obtain was not enough; thus, the study examiner was armed with other necessary tools required in the collection process.
4. **Data interpretation:** The most important aspect of the data collection was to determine the interpretation and analysis process because it is important to articulate how this information would be used to solve the research problems (Moustakas, 1994).

The study relied on face-to-face, semi-structured interview with each participant (Moustakas, 1994). In a qualitative study, interviews protocol as shown in Appendix C was crucial and allowed the research examiner to gain in-depth information about participants' experiences (Moustakas, 1994; Kvale, 2007). The use of interview questions proposed for this study met two criteria, (1) they provided the required data, and (2) generated such data that were comprehensible and analytical. Because researchers rely on extensive interviews in the phenomenological study, semi-structured, open-ended questions was used to obtain data from each study participant (Moustakas, 1994). The wordings in the open-ended interview were exceptionally structured. The researcher used identical questions worded in such a way that responses were open-ended. This allowed the study participants to give more information, and also allowed the researcher more room for follow-ups (Gall, Gall, & Borg, 2003).

Data collection generated transcribed information and field notes. The notes consisted of observations made by the study participants, including phrases, statements, and thoughts. Moustakas (1994) suggested that in addition to handwritten notes, researchers should record the interview process to instill accuracy in the process. The interviews for the current study were recorded on voice-recording audio. The interviews were conducted in the conference rooms of both Org. A and Org. B . The format for the interview protocol is shown in Appendix C. Strategies in the direction of conversation and interview were flexible. The interview stages involved three most fundamental suggestions found in the literature; (a) preparation, (b) constructing and use of effective research questions, and (c) implementation (Kvale, 2007). The study examiner collected the Informed Consent forms prior to the interview. Background materials about the participants, including demographic information formed a part of the data collection process. Modified van Kaam's method of analysis involving the use of audio documented interviews of the research participants was used to analyze the research study (Mousakas, 1994).

Interview Protocol

The study researcher scheduled an interview with each of the participant and discussed consent, confidentiality, and recording of the interview. The research study examiner thus adhered to other interview standards provided in Appendix C. The interview process shifted the research from seeing humans as numerical objects to a quest for knowledge generated between individuals, through conversations (Kvale 1996). Semi-structured interviews was used as a data-collection instrument. Researchers choosing the interview approach often consider two basic approaches, (1) the process is time-consuming, and this could discourage participants, and (2) the process is open to interviewer bias. The current study used standardized open-ended interviews because the characteristics dovetails the phenomenological method. The open-ended interview strategy enabled participants to answer the same questions, thereby increasing content comparability (Moustakas, 1994).

During the interview process, each of the participants were asked to think about their experience as a Nigerian living under the economic, political, social, and cultural system of various governmental regimes. Participants were also asked to think about the leaders who led through those regimes, and how their economic, political, social, and cultural system policies or management have influenced their livelihoods. The interviews aimed at uncovering the array of cognitive phases participants have experienced. The complete list of 13 interview questions posed to each participant are shown on Appendix D.

Instrument Selection Appropriateness

The current study depended almost exclusively on lengthy interviews, using open-ended and exploratory questions in a format that allowed participants to describe their thoughts and perceptions in their words (Moustakas, 1994). The semi-structured interview instrument was most appropriate for the current study because it allowed participants the flexibility to express their true feelings. This interview approach also allowed participants to provide realistic information about their observations, perceptions, and knowledge of the circumstance (Dreyfus & Wrathall, 2006). Each interview in the current study was tape recorded, transcribed, and thermalized (Moustakas, 1994).

The purpose of the qualitative phenomenological research study was to understand how political, cultural, social and economic conditions in Nigeria influence the lives of Nigerian citizens through lived experiences of two citizens from each of the six geopolitical regions of the country. The study central Research Question was: "How do Nigerian citizens describe their experience of living under economic, political, cultural, and social hardships?" Kvale (1996) noted that the development of interview questions should reflect the study purpose and the research question. Such interview questions must be objective, anonymous, and devoid of any emotions and subjective interests (Kvale, 1996). As shown in Appendix D, Questions one through twelve were intended to allow participants to describe their experience in their own words. Question thirteen was intended to allow participants the flexibility to share other relevant experience as they wish. The questions were structured in such to allow empirical data to "emerge" rather than "forcing" them (Bentz and Shapiro, 1998).

The use of several participants reduced interviewer effects and bias, and facilitated rich-tick data-collection process (Moustakas, 1994). This current study considered fundamental characteristics of qualitative research interviews suggested by Kvale (1996);

1. Researcher used natural language to involve, comprehend and interpret participants' lived experience.
2. Researcher explored and reveals the descriptions and meaning of participants' conditions and engagements, rather than generalities.
3. Researcher appeared thoughtful and open to new data

and phenomena.

4. Researcher was cognizant to possible vagueness and inconsistencies of participants' narrative.
5. Researcher adopted the interviews and relevant practices as an interpersonal encounter.

It could have been argued that the telephone interview that has long been recognized as a principal method of data collection would provide a similar need. For instance, Borg and Gall (1996) discussed several advantages associated with the telephone interviewing over a face-to-face process. These included; cheaper process and swifter responses, elimination of the cost and burden of transportation, and opportunity to recruit participants from a much spread-out population. Weisberg et al. (1996) however differed, suggesting that face-to-face interviews may be more suitable, especially where the interviewer wishes to discourse strong issues or address very complex questions. This study focused on the Nigerian citizens and their lived experience under a leadership condition, and aimed at a deeper and self-generated answers from participants. A natural setting, therefore yielded better accuracy (Seidman, 1991). The study's format for the interview process is provided in Appendix C.

Validity and Reliability

Validity in a research study primarily means truthfulness, whereas reliability indicates process consistency or dependability. The goal of every researcher is to strive for objectivity as well as avoid subjectivity at all costs (Moustakas 1994). Whereas observations should be least influenced, researchers aim at a study process not susceptible to their perceptions, impressions, and biases. Therefore, one basic way to remain objective is to create an efficient approach of measuring the validity and reliability of the phenomenon being studied. Patton (1990) hinted that there are no straightforward strategies to ensure the reliability and validity of qualitative research study, but cautioned that specific guidelines do exist. As effective validity guidelines, the current study focused on four primary areas, (1) credibility, (2) transferability, (3) reliability, and (4) conformability (Moustakas 1994; Denzin & Lincoln, 1994; Lincoln & Guba, 1985, 1989). The application of these practices in the current study are as follows;

1. **Credibility:** The study researcher demonstrated process credibility by establishing to participants, data confidentiality and strict honesty in data handling. The current study managed the accuracy of responses by routine collaboration with study participants during the interview process to verify responses and update field notes (Lincoln & Guba, 1985).
2. **Dependability:** Dependability in a research study is substantiated when conclusions are consistent and could be replicated (Lincoln & Guba, 1995). To illustrate dependability, substantiation of collected data, findings, interpretations, and recommendations must be established. The current study used reliable recording tools and detailed note-taking to ensure accurate transcriptions. To ensure accuracy the study used NVivo 10 ® Software to label, organize, and code relevant data that emerged from the participants' responses. (Moustakas 1994).
3. **Conformability:** In a qualitative study, conformability denotes the notion of objectivity and neutrality (Lincoln and Cuba, 1995). Validity can be established when

study conclusions aligns with the focus rather than the examiner biases (Denzin & Lincoln, 1994). The current study used comprehensive record-keeping and data preservation for possible scrutiny. These are fundamental strategies in establishing conformability. Audit-Trail suggested by Lincoln and Cuba (1995) also played significant role in the current study. A thorough preservation of records regarding all segments of this study process was proposed to allow any broad assessment of the research conduct.

4. **Transferability:** Transferability is established when study results are generalized to other conditions, populations, or situations (Lincoln and Cuba, 1995). A crucial distinction was made by Yin (2010) between "statistical generalizations" associated with the quantitative and "analytic generalization" focusing on typical qualitative approach. The current study could be generalized to populations other than Nigeria citizens currently living under a governmental system.

Internal Validity

Validity indicates "accuracy," whereas internal validity justifies the exactness within the study. The researcher must have substantial evidence of a correlation between the cause and effect. Thus, it is important that the projected variable is certainly the one affecting the outcomes (Moustakas, 1994). The internal validity measures relevant design and data so that the researcher could draw precise assumptions about content and analysis. To implant the process of internal validity and eliminate possible doubts about research accuracy, this study applied 'Member-Checking,' a process explained by

Moustakas (1994) as the most decisive method for establishing the credibility of data. This process shifted the validity procedure from the researcher to the participant. To authenticate this process, the researcher took data and interpretations back to the participants to rectify incoherencies and confirm the credibility of narrative responses.

A second application of validity was established by eliminating interview-interference from the research examiner (Salkind, 2002). Lincoln and Guba (1985) recommend using a field notebook to reduce subjectivity during the interview process. These are notes generated during the interviews to remember or track down significant comments that might contribute to or supplement the interview data. The process prioritized human factors and prevented unnecessary interruptions of the interview process (Lincoln & Guba, 1985).

External Validity

One of the primary goals of this study was to guarantee the external validity, and this was done by demonstrating the ability to generalize the findings (Kalaian, & Kasim, 2008). External validity indicates the potential for the study to apply the conclusions to other settings, populations, and times (Salkind, 2002; Thomas, 2005; Kalaian, & Kasim, 2008). The validity of a sample representative might pose a significant threat when results apply only to the sample rather than to the target population from which the sample was selected (Kalaian, & Kasim, 2008). To adequately establish process accuracy through external validity, this study considered the reduction of biases as an important element of carrying out a credible process (Yin, 2009). Biases were reduced because the study examiner had a good knowledge of the research subject to ensure that the appropriate questions were asked. In addition, the current study researcher applied good listening skills and remain composed to avoid influencing study participants in their responses (Yin, 2009).

Ethical Considerations

There are ethical-moral dimensions to every approach in social research. Ethics defines what is not appropriate or what is morally obligatory in research procedures. This process often leaves researchers with two conflicting values; a quest for scientific knowledge and the rights of participants. Ethical issues in research often arise from either of four concept classifications: "protection of harm, informed consent, right to privacy, and honesty with professional colleagues" (Sales & Folkman, 2000). The current study involved human beings who served as participants. However, the interview process did not warrant such participants' exposure to unnecessary physical or psychological harm. The research used Informed Consent explained earlier in this chapter to seek participation (van den Hoonaard & Will, 2002). To adhere to strict honesty with professional colleagues, the research reported all findings in a comprehensive and honest manner. No findings were misrepresented, and the researcher did not intentionally mislead others about the nature of the study results. Furthermore, there was no fabrication of data to support any of the conclusions.

To mitigate any possible ethical impropriety, this research study adhered to the fundamental regulatory principles specifically designed by the American Evaluation Association (AEA) to encourage best practices in the evaluation processes (Moseley & Dessinger, 2010);

1. **Systematic Inquiry:** Conducting systematic, data-based inquiries ensure the accuracy and credibility of the process. To adhere to this principle, the current study communicated all methods and approaches accurately, and in sufficient details to allow others to understand, interpret, and review the project.
2. **Competence:** This requires that researchers possess applicable training, and experience. To substantiate this principles, the study examiner possesses appropriate training, aptitudes, and experience through doctoral courses on research methods and processes to assume the duties projected in the study development.
3. **Integrity and Honesty:** This requires best practices in process engagements. The study examiner went beyond obtaining permission from research participants but also briefed each of them on the process demands to enable them make informed decisions.
4. **Respect for all People:** Research study process projects integrity when participants treated with respect and dignity. Hence, evaluation and results in the current study was communicated in a manner that respected individual dignity (Moseley & Dessinger, 2010).

Data Analysis

The current study adopted the tradition of the investigative process of the existential phenomenology (Merriam, 2009; Moustakas, 1995). The role of the study examiner must not be ignored in the research process. Whereas the quantitative researcher distances from the study participants, Moustakas (1994) notes that the qualitative researcher partners with participants. The concept of epoche played a substantial role during data collection and analysis. In the process, the researcher looked at the phenomenon with an open mind so as to acquire new knowledge of the essence of experience (Moustakas). The application of Epoche therefore helped to mitigate possible prejudgment and biases during the study process (Merriam, 2009; Moustakas, 1994). In achieving this purpose, the study examiner suspended every bias throughout the data collection and data analysis of the study process. The focus of the interview process in the current study was to collect the perceived lived experiences of Nigerian citizens living with political, cultural, social and economic uncertainty. Participant interviews and data collection was followed by content analysis of documents and audio-recorded information derived from the process.

Data analysis in the current study was performed with seven-step Modified van Kaam Method of Analysis of Phenomenological Data (Moustakas, 1994). The method was appropriate because it processed and presented the experiences of each participant within the Individual Structural and Textural-Structural descriptions. This helped the researcher to characterize the meanings of the participant's experiences (Moustakas, 1994). As shown in Figure 4, the application of seven-step modified van Kaam method in the current study are as follows;

1. **Reviewing and grouping:** Initial assessment and grouping enabled the identification and reporting of relevant comments made by research participants.
2. **Reduction and elimination of invariant themes:** This process entailed the removal of expressions considered irrelevant to the phenomenon.
3. **Theme-clustering and identification:** statements from

the lived experience were clustered into core themes within a particular topic.

4. **Validation of segments:** Statements and themes that were consistent with interview intent were validated. This confirmed that identified statements and themes were consistent with the complete record of the research participants.
5. **Development of Individual textural description:** All validated constituents and themes from study participants were constructed from textual descriptions of the experience.
6. **Creation of Individual textural description:** individually, participant's structural essence of the lived experience were constructed based on individual textural description and imaginative distinction.
7. **Construct essences of the experience:** Using the individual statements assigned to the specific themes, a textural-structural description of the meanings and essences of the experience was constructed (Moustakas, 1994).

The essential tasks in analyzing study data are to identify common themes when participants describe their experience. After the interview process, the audio recorded information was transcribed into the written document. The study examiner reviewed the textual data and sent them back to participants for review. This process finalized all updates and further validated the documents for secure storing and data-entry preparation process. The researcher developed and analyzed the themes, explored and documented descriptive experiences and meanings. NVivo data-analysis software procured for this research was equipped with texts, audio, and

Figure 4:

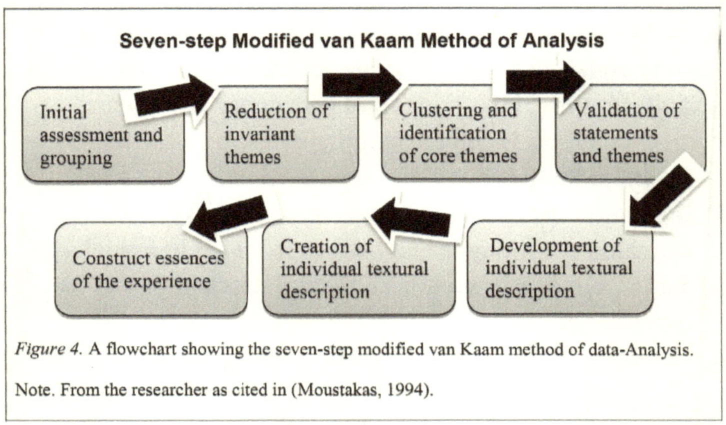

Figure 4. A flowchart showing the seven-step modified van Kaam method of data-Analysis.

Note. From the researcher as cited in (Moustakas, 1994).

video tools. Text files and audios in various formats were imported for transcriptions, and data sources were coded accordingly (Bassett, 2010). NVivo is Microsoft Word compatible and possesses other features that were applicable to this research design. For instance, exact text selections could be annotated from large documents, and color highlights were used to simplify readings and editing (Bassett, 2010).

Summary

Chapter 3 outlined the methodology design, data analysis, and ethical considerations of the proposed research study. The chapter also provided substantial justification on why the qualitative method was the most appropriate for the current research study. The purpose of the study is to understand how political, cultural, social and economic conditions in Nigeria influence the lives of Nigerian citizens through lived experiences of two citizens from each of the six geopolitical regions of the country. In-depth interviews were conducted to obtain data from Nigerians citizens currently living in the Nigeria. A qualitative study was suitable for this process because the approach among other features, focused on people and situations in real environments (Maxwell, 2005). Existential approach enabled the researcher to retrieve relevant descriptions of participants' experience, and their understanding of living in the system under study (Patton, 2002; Adams & Manen, 2008). The standard of shared experience synonymous with phenomenology thus dovetails the research purpose. Chapter 3 explored two fundamental purposes; (1) regulated data acquisition and (2) extracted meaning from them through strategic interpretation and analysis (Moustakas, 1994). Chapter 4 presented with detailed analysis; the research findings derived from data collection and analysis.

Chapter 4
Results

■ Analysis of data gathered from face-to-face interviews of 12 Nigerian citizens, two from each of the six geopolitical regions currently living through the system yielded five primary themes. The identified themes are as follows; (a) moral philosophy, (b) skills and training (c) ineffective management, and (d) politics and diversity. These themes helped to answer the research question.

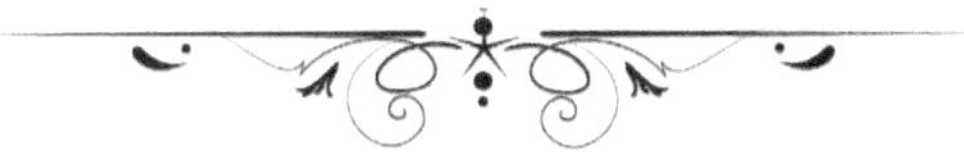

The purpose of the qualitative phenomenological research study was to understand how political, cultural, social and economic conditions in Nigeria influenced the lives of Nigerian citizens through lived experiences of two citizens from each of the six geopolitical regions of the country namely,

North-Central, North-Eastern, North-Western, South-Eastern, South-South, and South-Western regions. Chapter 3 consisted of the methodology used for the current research study. This included a description of the responsibility of the study researcher in handling each part of the process. These processes are, population, instrumentation, data collection, and the development of data analysis used in the study development. Other elements in the chapter comprised the sampling of research study participants, handling of the informed consent and confidentiality, internal and external validity, and reliability.

The study used a face-to-face, semi-structured interview to gain knowledge from 12 Nigerian residents who served as participants. The execution of the methodology process described in chapter 3 generated a total of 45 pages of transcribed data and 14 pages of field notes. Data generated from the interview process were classified into process codes and themes. The themes were gathered from relevant patterns established in the data presented by each of the research study participants. Data collection process, data analysis, identification of themes, and a summary of the findings were included in Chapter 4.

Data Collection Process

The study relied on face-to-face, semi-structured interview which lasted between 60 and 90 minutes in length with each participant. Study participants were drawn from two groups; Org. A and Org. B respectively. The initial participants' identification progressed with verification of basic demographics information to establish the appropriate geopolitical regions. Six participants were selected from each organization. At the end of the process, 12 participants, two citizens from each of the six Nigerian geopolitical regions were selected. The use of several participants reduced interviewer bias and facilitated rich-tick data-collection process. The use of semi-structured open-ended questions allowed participants the flexibility to express their true feelings. It also enabled them to provide realistic information about their personal experience of the circumstance.

Telephone contact numbers for each of the two groups, Org. A and Org. B were located on the public website through Google Search. The group leaders were initially reached through their phone contacts, and they agreed to announce the study to their members before and during their general meetings. All meetings were opened to every Nigerian as well as the public for networking. This enabled the study examiner to gain entrance into the meetings throughout the process. The study examiner interacted with members of both organization before or after each meeting. An official request forms shown in Appendix B were signed by the leaders to use their premises for the interview process. The study researcher visited the meeting locations after the request was granted and initiated the research process. Consent Forms, as shown in Appendix A, was handed over to the individuals who consented to take part in the study. Each of the participants signed the consent forms. The signed consent forms were collected from participants accordingly, and interview dates and times were scheduled. Each of the participants in the study received a copy of the signed Informed Consent Form on the scheduled day of the interview. The study examiner received the permission from each participant to digitally record the interviews.

To authenticate this process, the researcher took the transcribed data back to the participants to rectify incoherencies. Each participant agreed with the data composition as no objections, or additional comments were made. Each interview process adhered strictly to the research study interview protocol shown in Appendix C. Participants in the current study were briefed on the process to enable them make informed decisions. Participants were also adequately informed about their rights of confidentiality, which entailed protecting their names and other personal information from the study analysis. Among other stipulations, the informed content included the right of the participant to participate, decline, or withdraw from the study at any occasion. Participants were also informed that they should not be penalized for withdrawing from the study. Participants who would decide to withdraw from the research study were asked to contact the researcher through the contact phone number provided on the consent form.

Process confidentiality were clearly communicated to each study participant. Each of the participants was notified that the concealment of all subjects was to be assured through the use of secured log-ins, passwords, codes, and folders identifying individual matters. Participants were also informed that specific codes rather than their names would be used in the process. As shown in Figure 3, the six geopolitical zones were coded as follows: (1) North-Central: NC-1 and NC-2, (2) North-Eastern: NE-1 and NE-2, (3) North-Western: NW-1 and NW-2, (4) South-Eastern: SE-1 and SE, (5) South-South: SS-1 and SS-2, (6) South-Western: SW-1 and SW-2.

Confidentiality of data and information during the process was also communicated to participants. Interviews were recorded, transcribed and saved in the computer server protected with passwords and electronic file-backups. Access to the box would require numeric combination known to only the researcher. Original documents and all research data gathered in the interview process would be secured safely in a safe deposit box for a period of three years. Research data included notes taken during the interviews, transcripts, tape recordings, and text messages. After the three-year period, research documents would be shredded, and the electronic information permanently deleted from the system. Each participant was allowed the flexibility to ask questions related to the interview settings or process. A choice was also be provided to allow participants request for breaks during the process. The aforementioned processes were substantially communicated to each study participant, and no additional questions were asked.

The interviews were conducted in the conference rooms of both the Org. A and Org. B respectively. The interview process and sessions were recorded on voice-recording audio. The format for the interview protocol is shown in Appendix C. Data collection during the interview process generated transcribed information and field notes. The notes consisted of observations made by the study participants and included additional phrases and statements that were not substantially captured by the digital recorder. Data were transcribed at the end of every interview session. To guarantee accuracy of data transcription from the digital audio recorder to the computer system, the researcher executed a second run of the data transcription. This was followed by condensing of data generated from each participant. Data generated from the recorder were assessed and compared with the field notes to identify disparities or any additional information that were required for the study.

The researcher observed the willingness from each study participant to offer a descriptive answer to each of the questions asked during the interview process. Field notes observation indicated that participants were calm and composed during the interview process. The purpose of the current qualitative phenomenological research study was to understand how political, cultural, social and economic conditions in Nigeria influence the lives of Nigerian citizens through lived experiences of two citizens from each of the six geopolitical regions of the country. The research study question was: How do Nigerian citizens describe their experience of living under economic, political, cultural, and social hardships? The determination would generate a better understanding of the challenges Nigerian citizens living in the country face under their leadership conditions. Understanding leadership and how conditions in Nigeria influence the lives of Nigerian citizens through their lived experiences facilitated the discovery of new and constructive information that can provide recommendations for effective management of people, their differences, resources, and their aspirations.

Demographics

To align with this procedure, the sample size of the current study was 12 participants, drawn from two citizens from each of the six Nigerian's geopolitical regions categorized as, (a) North-Central, (b) North-Eastern, (c) North-Western, (d) South-Eastern, (e) South-South, and (f) South-Western (see Table 3). Drawing samples from each of the geopolitical zones increases the validity of the study in ensuring that findings are an accurate representation of the phenomena. Variations in qualitative methodologies can affect the concept of data saturation in qualitative study (Kvale, 1996). The phenomenon can also detects both the method, scope, and the kind of participants (Hycner, 1999). The concept of data saturation adopted by the current study set a limit for capacity of the needed data (Kvale, 1996; Seidman, 2006). The study examiner interacted and recruited participants continually until the appropriate sample size was reached. An applicable sample size for a qualitative study provides satisfactory answers to the research question. A typical sample size is from 5 to 25 interviewees with direct experience in the study area (Moustakas, 1994).

Interviews were conducted with participants drawn from visiting Nigerians citizens who attend monthly meetings of Org. A and Org. B respectively. The study examiner selected purposive sampling because it is considered the most effective non probability approach to identifying the primary participants (Welman & Kruger, 1999; Moustakas, 1994). During the recruitment exercise, a total of three participants were left out of consideration because the maximum number of their zones of origin were reached. One participant withdrew because of conflict of interests that arose from parliamentary involvement. The process proceeded with personal interaction and chats until a total of 12 potential participants were reached. Six participants were selected from each group, with two citizens each representing each of the six Nigerian's geopolitical regions. Table 3 shows participants' demography listed in the order which the interviews were conducted. The age and gender of each participant were recorded for identification purposes and have played no other role in the research study.

Table 3.

Participants' Demographics

Zones	Codes	Gender	Zones	Codes	Gende
North-Central	NC-1	Male	South-Eastern	SE-1	Male
	NC-2	Male		SE-2	Femal
North-Eastern	NE-1	Female	South-South	SS-1	Male
	NE-2	Male		SS-2	Femal
North-Western	NW-1	Female	South-Western	SW-1	Femal
	NW-2	Male		SW-2	Male

Data Analysis

Data-reporting process entails a systematic review of transcripts, identification of relevant units, textural-structural description, and composite textural-structural descriptions. Transcripts were thoroughly examined by both study researcher and individual participants for accuracy. Participants were satisfied with the content and did not make any changes or corrections. This transcript examination process was considered a validation of the descriptions and demonstration of the true essence of their experiences. To enable the study researcher understand the experience of each participant comprehensively, the practice of Epoche' was applied during reading and transcription of interview responses. The application of Epoche mitigated possible prejudgment and biases during the study process (Merriam, 2009; Moustakas, 1994). In achieving this purpose, the study examiner suspended every bias throughout the process of data analysis.

Data analysis for the current research study sought to filter through the rich description of data generated during the interview process, code them, and categorize them into themes. The current study used NVivo 10 ® Software to label, organize, and code relevant data that emerged from the participants' responses. Automatic coding of relevant words, phrases, and sentences was used to generate most relevant themes. The system application allowed data to be substantially grouped and relinked into meaning and description. The grouping were compared with each other and consolidated until no other data or themes developed. Figure 5 comprised comprehensive themes that emerged from the categories, namely: (a) moral philosophy (b) skills and training (d) ineffective management, and (e) politics and diversity. The comprehensive themes were used to corroborate the study findings.

Findings

Analysis of data gathered from face-to-face interviews of 12 Nigerian citizens, two from each of the six geopolitical regions currently living through the system yielded five primary themes. The identified themes are as follows; (a) moral philosophy, (b) skills and training (c) ineffective management, and (d) politics and diversity. These themes presented in the following section helped to answer the research question: How do Nigerian citizens describe their experience of living under economic, political, cultural, and social hardships?

Figure 5

Figure 5. Flow chart shows comprehensive themes that emerged from codes and categories of words, phrases, and texts. The comprehensive themes were used to corroborate the study findings.

Note. Flowchart prepared by the researcher.

Theme 1: Moral Philosophy. This theme, Moral Philosophy is the application of rules and values in making decisions about what is right or wrong. All the 12 participants, when asked how they felt about their leaders, expressed concerns about widespread corruption among them. Phrases and sentences were dominated by words such as dishonest, fraud, embezzlement, bad leaders, bribery, and corruption. Many of participants believed that a reduction of fraud in the public service would usher in a new system whereby the citizens could once again trust their leaders. Collectively, their experi-

ence in the system, and their observation reflect some negative attitudes. SE-1 described their leaders as "Incompetent, corrupt, selfish, and greedy." NC-2 who visited the United States for an oil and gas related venture talked passionately about how corruption in Nigeria has been affecting international business, stating:

> I feel disappointed about our leaders because they allowed too much corruption to thrive. Now whenever we travel, we are looked at as corrupt people. At the foreign airports, at international fairs and seminars, the stories about Nigerians are the same – fraud, corruption, bribery and so on, and it get worse and worse. I came to the United States to source a company to partner with us to be doing contracts in Nigeria. We are into fabricating covers for oil storage tanks – but to my disappointment, I have to travel seven hours to Lubbock, Texas for minor meetings because potential clients could not attend to me on the phone. I felt the lack of trust, and the nonchalant attitude I was greeted with just because I am a Nigerian. I came back and called another company in Corpus Christi, and received a similar treatment. The message is simple: that we are corrupt people, and that the world have lost trust in us. And the bad thing is that the government are not adequately addressing these issues.

NC-1, who also visited the United States for an energy-related conference, narrated the negative implications of widespread corruption in Nigeria to international commerce and had this to say:

> I think that those corrupt Nigerian public servants and those internet scammers do not understand how bad

> they have damaged the image of our country. Last year, my partners in China withdrew our credit privileges and refused to send our supplies unless we wire physical cash. I am here in Houston for this reservoir simulation symposium, and it has been difficult trying to make meaningful contacts for my business and profession. The most we get is just complimentary cards from delegates because most delegates from other countries would not take us serious. A delegate actually asked me what I think about Nigeria being associated with international scam. I believe that our government needs to step up and address this issue because it is affecting international trade.

Some participants, however, did not generalize the entire system as 'corrupt' but recounted that there were instances where integrity prevailed. For instance, SE-2 believed that good managers and effective management existed in Nigeria with the exception of a few dishonest ones. SE-2 thinks that categorizing the entire country as "corrupt" would be misleading, because there were some leaders actually working diligently within the boundaries of the law and ethics. SW 1 echoed a similar sentiment, stating:

> Corruption is not everywhere as it seems in Nigeria. That is why I feel both proud and also so disappointed about my leaders, depending on which leader and which circumstance. There are good leaders who lead very well, and there are bad and corrupt leaders giving us a bad name. I believe that some of our leaders are so corrupt that they ignore the citizens who elected them and the purpose they were elected. The current leaders to my understanding are not that corrupt, but where I

> blame them is that they are not seriously tackling the rate of bribery and corruption in the country. For example, the police at the road checkpoints still take bribes from the motorist; an average staff at the airports, post offices and other public places still would take bribes to do his or her job. In the long run, what do we have? A society where bribery and corruption reign supreme.

NW-1 expressed a similar experience with corruption in public places through a different perspective, blaming the habit to economic hardship. According to NW-1, bribery and corruption are associated with unemployment, low salaries, and high prices of commodities in the midst of economic hardship. NW-1 stated:

> I understand that corruption is not something anybody, including me, would defend, but I have also observed that some people who engage in such practices are often left with no choice in trying to make ends meet. I am looking at an average policeman on the road who has a wife and many children but are underpaid, or civil servants who have to make ends meet with little salaries, but sometimes are not even paid. I am saying this because I am not a poor person, but I still find it hard sometimes to cope. It is always easy to condemn corruption, but if the government can effectively close the gap between the rich and poor by providing jobs and building a good economy where an average citizen would suffer less, the issue of bribery and corruption will reduce drastically.

NE-1 noted that corruption is rampant in the country because the leaders are corrupt, stating that erasing corruption can only be effective if it starts from the top. NE-1 stated:

> If leaders who are supposed to build our roads, give us lights and other amenities embezzle the funds, what do you expect from their followers? In Nigeria, there is this thing called "kickback" which is just another name for bribery in civil service. Government contractors usually spend an enormous amount of money offering kickbacks to top government officials and by the time the get the contracts, there would not be enough money to carry it out. This is why today, we don't have roads – no lights and no electricity. Contractors are only after the profit while the citizens are left without showing them any amenities for their taxes. This is horrible.

A few participants (NE-2, SS-1, SS-2, and SE-1) attributed poor leadership in Nigeria to a high rate of corruption that governs the electoral process. The observation was that wrong leaders are ushered into the workforce through the backdoor, therefore, pervading the entire system with underhandedness and incompetency. SS-1 stated:

> We must understand that corruption is not just taking bribes, and stealing. Most elections I have witnessed in Nigeria are either rigged or canceled. And by the time you know, the positions are all filled up with strange people who cannot perform. This again goes back to the government because they are responsible for conducting the process. But what do you have? The same agencies that are conducting the election are also doing the rigging. With what I have seen in Nigeria, I believe that the entire system in corrupt – everybody including those in government.

SS-1 drew a significant comparison between Nigeria and

Houston, Texas where he is visiting for the first time based on various observations:

> I have been here for just about a week and have observed that good behavior is not just for the leaders but for all and sundry. I was surprised that even at the airports, the supermarkets, and other public places I passed through, the staffs were very professional and well behaved. In my country, the airport workers demanded bribes even to check in my baggage at the airport. Some of them even made notes on when I am coming back and asked me to buy things for them from America. This is how far corruption has spread in our public system. Even our behaviors at public places are nothing to write home about. The experienced I encountered from the offices I visited to make inquiries for my computer business in Lagos showed me that honesty in the society starts from our behavior or attitude as human beings. My president is not the one to tell me that I should wait for my turn in the banks and post offices to be attended to. My state governor is not the one to tell me that it is wrong to demand money or bribe from a citizen to render him the service I am employed for. My parish priest is not the one to tell me that it is immoral to take money from the government to do contract and embezzle it. So what you have in Nigeria is a corruption problem that is spreads across the board, and not just among the leaders.

Interview questions 2 and 3 which asked participants to describe how they felt about their government and how they felt about their leaders respectively drew so many responses about the prevalence of corruption in the region. Whereas most participants agreed on a high level of corruption in the system A few participants however, recounted that there were instances where integrity prevailed in the system. Besides a countenance reflecting feelings of dissatisfaction, each participant accentuated disappointment and a loss of confidence in their leaders in curbing corruption.

Theme 2: Skills and Training. This theme, Skills and Training, relates to development of abilities, and individual capacity to manage tasks as well as rise up to imminent challenges. As the interviews and gathering of data progressed, participants spoke vastly about values of education and knowledge in the Nigeria's public service system. In Interview Questions 5, 7, 9, and 11 asking participants to describe how they felt about the political, economic, social, and cultural process in Nigeria, responses focused on inadequacies in managing skills. Many responses were overwhelmed with words and phrases reflecting incompetence, lack of knowledge, inefficiency, and insufficient training in the public system. Participants spoke vehemently about how the public service system were staffed with managers and leaders who lacked relevant knowledge about their respective designations.

SE-1, SE-2, and SW-1 individually noted that the type of leaders Nigeria have produced in the past and present have been major factors for the current management insufficiencies facing the system. SW-1 further stressed that the current state of the nation being unable to live up to the expectations of the citizens were an accumulation of problems that developed over time. According to SW-1:

> If you observe the caliber of leader we have had since

> 1960, you would agree that the major issues we face today started a long time ago. For example, most of the leaders that governed our country, our states, and major corporations were not properly trained to handle those responsibilities. Some of the elected one got in through rigged elections while the appointed ones made it through their godfathers or based on their tribal origin. How do we explain the scenario where a whole president of the most populous country in Africa, or a governor does not have basic education? It has happened in Nigeria – quote me.

SE-2 held a similar view and stressed that among all Nigerian leaders since its independence in 1960, only the late President Umaru Musa Yar'Adua and the incumbent, President Goodluck Jonathan had college degrees. A situation SE-2 said, led to an accumulation of failures in policy making and national development. SE-2 stated:

> The illiterates that led us in the past created the foundation to our present problem. I am not trying to criticize people for a lack of education or something, but I believe that certain jobs and positions require certain qualifications. Nigeria has always used a so-called quota system of tribes and zones to staff their federal personnel rather than the required skills and knowledge. Qualification is crucial because it creates opportunities for good service and progress. Do you know that since 1960, the only time a well-educated Nigerians have ruled this country was the regime of the late President Yar'Adua, and the current regime of President Jonathan? When I say well-educated, I mean, at least a president with a university degree. This may

> sound ridiculous but if you look at these facts, you understand why at this point, it's hard to manage this country. The damage done in the past is so destroying that it would take more labor to repair it.

In further discussions about skills and competencies, participants spoke about years of the military regime in Nigeria. SE-1 cited a string of military coups and dictatorship as an example of a situation where the wrong leaders imposed themselves on the followers for the wrong reasons. SE-1 stated:

> If you look at the number of coups that we have had and the number of officers that have imposed themselves as our leaders, it will be easier to imagine why we are in such a mess. These are military officers without adequate training to govern – and in the long run we are left with a country with talents, good resources, and the worst economy. My point is not just the fact that these officers were not trained to manage the country, but also that anytime there is a coup; there is a setback. In other words, those leaders have only succeeded in setting us back politically, economically, socially, and culturally.

SW-2 also spoke substantially about the string of military regimes that interrupted Nigeria's leadership development, and noted:

> Not giving democracy a chance to thrive by army officers who lacked the skills to manage our natural resources, sociopolitical development, and our cultural differences is what I think that kept us in our current situation. I used to praise the military when I was young as the messiah to our problems, as they would

> always mention corruption in government as reasons for military coups. Well, that was what they made us believe, and that was the impression we have always had. Make no mistake – the problems we have today in Nigeria were created by those horrible moments.

NC-1, NC-2, and NW-1 in their individual responses addressed the issue of skills and competence from a different perspective. They emphasized that so much attention to issues of skills and competence without a structure that integrates all geographical zones in the leadership process would be disenfranchising. NC-1 stated:

> I understand the need for skills and competence in managing our country, but there are other important factors we must consider. Using only our level of education to determine who leads where or who manages would just elevate some areas as well as marginalize others. From my observation, the problem is that Nigeria has not created that structure where every region would have equal opportunities for educational training and development. Until such a time, it must set a standard that does not isolate those citizens failed by the system.

NW-1 criticized the present Nigerian leaders for paying so much attention to academic degrees, while other areas of managing the needs of their citizens were undermined. NW-1 stressed that the nature of Nigeria's geographical and cultural terrain requires other management strategies besides scholarly accolades. NW-1 stated:

> Look at the United States, for instance, there are policies in place to accommodate, all ethnicities – the Blacks, women, and other groups historically held back

> by the system. In the Nigeria culture, women are in most cases downgraded to the background. Some tribes are historically disadvantaged by a lack of civilization and government presence, so how do we accommodate them? These and many other issues are what we should put into consideration to achieve any progress in Nigeria.

Theme 3: Ineffective Management. This theme, Ineffective Management, relates to total lapses in effective management. Interview Questions 4, 6, 8, 10, and 12 inquired how the leadership, as well as political, economic, social, and cultural processes, were affecting the quality of their lives as Nigerians. The issues of unemployment, lack of amenities, lapses in basic development, and economic hardship dominated all responses. All 12 participants individually expressed disappointment with their past and present leaders over what they attributed to lapses in effective resources management. SE-2 stated:

> I don't know where to start but in my country we are living in hardship. I am not talking about citizens living big in the townships – I am talking about my family members in the villages and other struggling masses who do not have access to basic live amenities. The government cannot provide us with drinking water; they cannot provide us with good roads; they cannot provide us with good hospitals. Take the roads, for example – the only road leading to my village is a death trap, ruining vehicles and causing accidents and lives.

SS-1 noted that government's inability to address a pervasive nonexistence of basic needs for a long period have made them lose hope in their leaders. The study researcher observed an expression of emotional deportment as SE-2 narrated the prevailing lived-in condition:

> The horrible thing is that we still have leaders in the absence of everything that taxpayers are entitled to. I have relatives that graduated from the universities two to three years now who are still looking for jobs. The good-paying government jobs are reserved for the well-to-dos while others are left helpless. I have a son going to school in Ghana now because he could not find admission in Nigeria, and there are thousands of Nigerians overseas just to attend school. And the funny thing is that our politicians and leaders would always tell us about change and transformation, so where is the change? Where is it? Where is the transformation?

The demonstrative atmosphere during interview responses about public amenities, again manifested when SW-1 spoke about how a loved one died during childbirth because of inadequate medical facility. It was a solemn moment of the interview engagement – the reality of the phenomenological experience where participants unleashed their experiences in their words. This was how SW-1 explained her experience:

> Talk about amenities – this is the area I try not to address because it reminds me of a terrible ordeal two years ago. Anyway, since you also asked me how the leadership and the social processes are affecting the quality of my life as a Nigerian citizen, I will be glad to let it out. I lost my niece last year while she was giving birth to her first child. I know that doctors were on strike during that time. The story was that something went wrong during delivery and she needed blood, but

> there was none. My niece died, but her baby survived. May her soul rest in peace.

Interview responses relating to inadequate healthcare and other amenities did not end with SW-1. Every participant was so detailed about their experience living in Nigeria under a leadership structure faulted by political, economic, social, and cultural uncertainties. NC-1 described how his father frequented London for treatment for years before he finally died. NC-1 stated:

> The issue of our government and social service management in my country is terrible, especially in the area of health. I am lucky because I have this opportunity to be in America every year, so I use that chance to do my medical checkup, then buy all the medicine that my mom needs, but this is not the case here. The issue is that the processes you are asking about do not even exist. I lost my father last year to prostate cancer, but before then, I and my siblings would contribute money every year to send him to London where my elder sister lived for either checkup or treatment. So where is the government? In as much as I still love my country, I will tell you sincerely that I do not have any leaders.

SE-1 was very categorical in denouncing Nigeria's political process, blaming the calamity to a lack of effective leadership and management. To corroborate his account, SE-1 compared Nigeria to other regions. Here is the response:

> The political process is useless. Nigerians need to understand the true definition of democracy before the political process can be effective. We need to initiate a standard for a certain pedigree of brilliant and foresighted individuals to be elected officials. For in-

> stance, the birth of the nation Dubai. When the Prince conceived the notion for a futuristic city, it was one that was voted impossible. Today it is a reality comes true. We need to follow the trend to catch up with the sequence of events; we need futuristic minds to position us among the G8. Nigeria has been blessed abundantly with great minds and resources, but the hooligans in power have brought us to ruins.

Other participants made similar observations about how deplorably, the political, economic, social, and cultural processes were affecting the quality of their lives, citing the issues of leadership and management as the major reasons. NC-1 also spoke critically:

> Our leadership is consistently ruining every aspect of growth for everyone. Greed and selfishness have led to the insurgency of this terrorist group called Boko Haram. Take a preview of the Nigeria's constitution and explain to me why certain leaders like State Governors should be given immunity during the course of their tenure. One of the most constraining problems of Nigeria is dichotomy. Rather than seeking ways to elevate the poverty in Nigeria, the entire country has been in a panic for the unknown.

Theme 4: Politics and Diversity. Theme, Politics and Diversity, relates to the application of politics in managing people and demographics, resources, culture and diversity. Matters of diversity dominated questions 11 and 12 asking participants to describe how they felt about Nigeria's cultural process, and how it was affecting the quality of their lives. Responses centered on dichotomy among tribes and regions;

a high level of tribalism, and inability of the leaders to develop the richness of Nigeria's culture. All the participants, except SE-1, believed that the complexities of Nigeria's multi-tribal cultural structure could be managed to benefit the country. SE-1, who described himself as a devoted Christian, revealed that most cultures in Nigeria are too outdated for a new world. According to SE-1:

> Rubbish culture that has failed to determine good from evil, right from wrong. It is just a failed practice. It has failed to improve anyone's life. Any system that is void of modification is a failed system that adds no human value.

On the influence of culture to the quality of lives of citizens, SE-1 held on to a spiritual belief and denounced the traditional lifestyle and culture as outdated and valueless. Citing the Holy Bible as a point of reference, SE-1 stated:

> In the book of Philippians 3:13, it is clearly stated, "Forget the past and look forward to what lies ahead." Cultural processes have not added value to anyone's livelihood.

However, SW-1's experience of the Nigerian multiple cultures revealed a different perspective. SW-1 attributed lapses in moral standards in the society to a lack of respect for individual cultures. SW-1 stated:

> From my experience as a Nigerian, I believe that we need our cultures because each of them carries numerous values that can make our families, towns, governments, and country better. Unfortunately, the present cultural process is messed up. You see where rich people with their ill-gotten wealth undermine the authorities of traditional rulers. I feel ashamed to say this, but

no one respects his elders anymore. Cultural management should start from home. If it cannot work in the homes, then it cannot work in the country. My philosophy is that when elders are not respected, they withhold their wisdom and the youth wallow in their ignorance, and the cycle continues ad infinitum.

SE-2 expressed the richness in cultural diversity but blamed the process lapses on a failure by the leaders to systematically manage Nigeria's multi-ethnicities. SE-2 stated:

> Think about America and how they legislate laws to manage diversity, and then one would agree that in our country, the issues of tribalism, inter-religious and inter-tribal fights can be adequately managed. Do we have rich cultures? Yes, but we have not used them to our advantage. The Hausa man wants to favor Hausas, and the Igbo person wishes to please his people, and so is Yoruba, as so on. The cultural process could have been one of the things that keep the citizen together but because we have not properly integrated our tribes and languages, our politics are compromised. To make this work, the leaders have to introduce programs that would eliminate the cultural division.

NC-2 echoed a similar sentiment blaming a prevalent discrimination in the public service to favoritism borne out of cultural and tribal affiliations. NC-2 stated:

> Our rich cultures are the only thing we should have been proud of, but we use it to divide ourselves. In the public service system, people get employment based on whom they know or whom they are related to. When I finished my secondary school years back, I remember how I was rejected for clerical jobs, even with my good school cer-

> tificate results. At the same time, I saw others being employed with written referral notes. Even when I was finally employed at the National Electric Power Authority (NEPA), it was my uncle who knew the district manager that helped me. In other words, there is tribalism and favoritism in every corner of the government. The North favors the north, the east favors the East and so on. Favoritism, tribalism, have destroyed our rich culture, and these have brought in unqualified labor force into the system because everybody tries to favor his or her own. This goes back to the issue of having unqualified leaders managing our resources.

SW-1 talked about the dangers of sectarian differences in a Nigeria's multicultural structure. As a Christian, SW-1 elaborated her experience having lived in parts of the country where Muslims were dominant. SW-1 stated:

> I am a Yoruba, and if there is anything we cherish so much it is our culture. But for the entire country, there are many cultures, and these have made peace and harmony impossible. I cannot travel to the Northern part now because there are religious unrests. I used to live in Jos, but my ordeal living there as a Christian totally changed me as a person. Simply, I made up my mind afterward that I will never live in a non-Christian community again. It is unfortunate that our cultures have divided us into tribes and religion. Right now, I do trust my Muslim brothers because of too many killings in the north. This is how the cultural process is affecting my life as a citizen.

NE-2 expressed optimism about overcoming a thread of ethnic rivalries and tribal sentiments, citing intermarriages as a practical non-political remedy. NE-2 said:

> We have a rich culture. I feel good about the diversity in our culture because it makes us more diversity and stronger. Also, I am a living testimony to the positive aspect of Nigeria's cultural process. It has impacted the quality of my life as a citizen because my relations are all married from different tribes and cultures. I am from Bauchi, North-East, and my wife is from Calabar, South-South. My brother is married to a fine Igbo woman from Aba, South-East. I speak three major Nigerian languages – Igbo, Hausa, and Yoruba – because I have lived in those places. I also have friends and relations in those areas. This is the richness of my country's culture. No matter how bad we may talk about our culture, I am very hopeful that it is working, at least through intermarriages.

NW-1 and NW-2 equally spoke on the trivialities of tribal differences, religious unrest, and favoritism in the Nigeria's cultural process, but expressed optimism for better prospects. NW-1 said, "I do not have any influence, so I am one of those bearing the burden of our cultural diversity, but all the same, we still have one of the best cultures in the world." NW-2 cited inter-cultural activities introduced by the past governments as another strategy to bridge the ethnic divides in the country. NW-2 stated:

> In Nigeria, we used to have different types of national and state cultural festivals where all ethnicities integrated. There were also other exchange programs where different tribes are brought together to share their rich cultures through art-related activities. We do not see these things these days, and this is why most of

the times we blame our problems on our leaders.

As the interview progressed, the influence of organizational politics in governance manifested with significant themes; nepotism, resources, marginalization, and patriotism. These themes also dominated participants' answers to questions 1 and 13 respectively. Question 1 inquired how participants felt about being Nigerians while 13 asked them to share their basic experience of living in Nigeria. All participants expressed love for their country Nigeria with enthusiasm. The words "love" and "patriotism" were used interchangeably as they expressed in their words, the joy of their citizenries. However, most of them expressed dissatisfaction with the leadership and management of resources. For instance, SS-1 stated:

> In as much as I love my country, I am still worried that since independence in 1960, some areas, especially in the geographical zone I belong, are still marginalized in allocation of resources. I come from a region where we are mainly minorities, and we produce crude oil that sustains the entire country, but over the years, since independence, we have been marginalized and were excluded from sharing the national cake. We are happy that the current President, Goodluck Jonathan is a minority – the first minority president since our independence. Now I feel confident because every tribe, regions, zones should be part of this process.

SS-2 expressed similar thoughts about how the politics of resources management in the country have been dominated by favoritism and marginalization. SS-2 also spoke about a connection between the patriotism and satisfaction as citizens, stating:

> I love Nigeria, but I don't know about patriotism yet until the leaders begin to care for my people. I feel that the economic process has been very selective. The area producing the resources were left underdeveloped during the majority areas siphon the national wealth. This is how I feel and until we all have equal opportunity in receiving the dividend of our economic resources, our love for our country will never be the same. Right now, the government are making changes but we see how long that lasts.

In response to question 1 asking how participants feel about being Nigerian citizens, SW-1 sang the country's national anthem as a mark of love and patriotism. SW-1 stated:

> Nigeria - my fatherland, the land of my birth, the land and people that influenced me during my formative years. I remember when we used to sing the national anthem in school, most especially during my elementary school years. With my hands on my chest, I would raise my voice to sing out it aloud "Arise oh, Compatriots!" This is the country I come from, and this is where I belong.

SW-2 expressed in details, an uneven distribution of resources in the country, blaming the practice on the aftermath of undemocratic structures initiated and operated by a thread of military regimes. SW-2 stated:

> I strongly think that the distribution of wealth in Nigeria is still partial. I am not going to mention names, but ever Nigerian knows that just a few areas enjoy the resources and development while others suffer. This issue I believe was created by the military regimes we had in the past. About being a Nigerian, I think that our gov-

> ernment treats the possession of citizenship lightly in Nigeria, which is sad! My thought is this: if you love Nigeria, take pride in being a Nigerian first! Forget the titles and the tribes.

NC-2 indicated that being a citizen of Nigeria means being patriotic and fulfilling every civic responsibility as a citizen. The participant also indicated that Nigeria would fare better, electing honest leaders with better approaches to handling the people and the resources. "Right now that is not the case so we shall keep praying," NC-2 concluded. NE-1, NW-1, and NC-2 also expressed dissatisfied with the resources management in the country blaming it on leaders who only serve their basic interest. NC-2 stated:

> I wouldn't blame it on any particular regime because if you rightly look at it, you would notice that every single regime including the present government is guilty of favoring one group or the other. It is a culture that has been there from the beginning. We must not address it by pointing fingers, but by starting to think and look at ourselves as Nigerians first before our zones, tribes, and political interests.

Besides the expression of love for their country, all the Nigeria citizens interviewed as participants agreed on the values of moral ethics, competence, and diversity in managing people and resources. Individual participants poured out their minds with 'thick-rich' descriptions about how the political, economic, social, and cultural processes in Nigeria influence their lives as citizens. The remarkable moments of the interview process were the disposition and sentiments that sometimes overwhelmed descriptive countenances of respective participants. An environment which is consistent with interpersonal connection built into the phenomenological process. A process, according to Van Manen (1990), which may not have been achieved through counting of figures, classification of geometric features or construction of statistical models as apply in the quantitative study approach.

Summary

Data collection for the current study started in February 2015 and lasted until March 2015. The research process entailed population-identification process, obtaining permission to use the premises, and a commitment to purposive sampling method. Other activities included collecting informed consent documents from study participants, scheduling and conducting face-to-face interviews, data collection and analysis and, and finally, the arrangement of data through the identified themes. 12 participants, two citizens from each of the six Nigerian's geopolitical regions categorized as, (a) North-Central, (b) North-Eastern, (c) North-Western, (d) South-Eastern, (e) South-South, and (f) South-Western participated individually in the semi-structured interviews. As shown in Figure 6, four comprehensive themes emerging from the grouping, analysis, and the synthesizing of data generated from participants' lived experience helped to answer the research question: How do Nigerian citizens describe their experience of living under economic, political, cultural, and social hardships? The comprehensive themes were: moral philosophy, (b) skills and training, (c) ineffective management, (d) politics and diversity.

In chapter 4, the study researcher explained the grouping, analysis, and the synthesizing of data according to the modified vann Kaam method (Moustakas, 1994). Data-reporting process entailed a systematic review of transcripts, identification of relevant units, textural-structural description, and composite textural-structural descriptions. Finally, a composite thematic textural-structural description was presented with a diagrammatic depiction of the lived experience of Nigerian citizens living through a political, cultural, social, and economic conditions. Chapter 5 provides in details, the study findings and magnifies further discoveries on the development of leadership as a solution to challenging trends in management. The findings are individually analyzed in relations to data previously presented, whereas each theme was methodically deliberated to inspire further development in management through effective leadership.

Figure 6

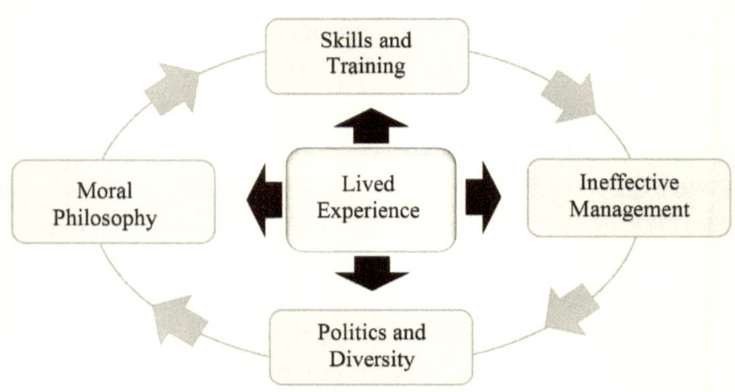

Figure 6. A flow chart showing a summary of comprehensive themes emerging from the grouping, analysis, and the synthesizing of data generated from participants' lived experience. The themes were used to corroborate the research findings and recommendations.

Note. Flowchart prepared by the researcher.

Chapter 5
Conclusions and Recommendations

■ The recommendations for leaders focused primarily on the themes identified in the current study. They are categorized under moral philosophy, organizational change, transformation, and diversity management. These remedies can help the present and aspiring leaders to develop effective leadership strategies to manage their citizens, public service system, and resources.

One of the keys to an organization's long-term success is effective leadership (Gallos, 2006, 2007; DeGeorge, 2010; Jones, 2010). Hence, modern-day leaders must be equipped with relevant competencies to meet the needs and aspirations of their citizens (Yukl, 2013). In Nigerian, the leadership is flawed and exacerbates the political, economic, cultural and social problems which directly influence the way citizens experience living in Nigeria (Abdullahi, Yahya, & Yelwa, 2012). This created extraordinary social problems unbearable to the citizens (Odunsi, 1996). Citizens suffer from economic deprivation despite the fact that the country is endowed with enough natural resources to boost its economic and sociopolitical management (Lawal, Imokhuede, & Johnson, 2012). Unfortunately, the need to develop relevant leadership knowledge in the Nigerian governmental system receives little or no attention (Lawal, Imokhuede, & Johnson, 2012).

The purpose of the qualitative phenomenological research study was to understand how political, cultural, social and economic conditions in Nigeria influenced the lives of Nigerian citizens through lived experiences of two citizens from each of the six geopolitical regions of the country namely, North-Central, North-Eastern, North-Western, South-Eastern, South-South, and South-Western regions. The study process was grounded on the rationale that qualitative researchers seek substantial knowledge to describe the existing phenomenon (Moustakas, 1994). The process captured the lived experiences of the study participants by engaging them in complex situations and interactions (Moustakas, 1994). In alignment with the qualitative culture, the interview method was appropriate to gather participants' true feelings about the circumstance (Dreyfus & Wrathall, 2006).

Chapter 4 explained the process of data-collection used to gather information from 12 Nigerian citizens who served as study participants. The chapter described with a detailed investigation, the analysis; identification of themes, and a summary of the findings. Analysis of data gathered from face-to-face interviews of the study participants yielded five primary themes namely; (a) moral philosophy, (b) skills and training (c) ineffective management, and (d) politics and diversity. Chapter 5 provides a summary of four proceeding chapters. The chapter also provides detailed discussions about the study limitations, implications and conclusions. The chapter also included the implication of the study of management in organizational leadership, and recommendations both for leaders, and future research.

Review of Previous Chapters

Chapter 1 presented a synopsis of the study's content, narrated the general problem, and explained the specific problem statements. Using the purpose statement, the chapter established the justification for the study, its consequences in Nigeria's governance processes, and significance in the study of leadership. The general problem addressed was that the quality of life that the citizens of the country experience is dependent on the leadership and when the governance is flawed, the citizens may suffer. The specific problem under study was that the Nigerian governance was flawed and exacerbates the political, economic, cultural and social problems which directly influence the way its citizen's experience living in Nigeria. In Chapter 1 also, the significance and nature of the study, as well as the theoretical framework that supported the study process were explained. The quest of the study was based on insufficient information available in the existing studies regarding how Nigerian citizens experience living through their governance system. By studying lived experiences of Nigerian citizens living through a governance phenomenon, findings, could strategically help the present and future leaders in countries struggling with resources management. This would help such leaders to direct a constructive performance intervention of startling governance anguishes. The present study could also reveal an insightful understanding of Nigeria's management process, the underperformances, and implications. It could add new information to existing knowledge of the practice of management in organizational leadership, and structures of the Nigerian governmental system. Also addressed in the chapter were definition of terms relevant to the leadership and management disciplines, assumptions, scope, limitations, and delimitations of the study.

Chapter 2 explained the literature review of the study – incorporating a broad examination of relevant texts that guided the process. The review revealed historical literatures associated with related concepts of the study's theoretical framework. Content included a comprehensive investigation of relevant texts that offered insight into past and present leadership processes in Nigeria; literature that discussed political, economic, cultural, and social development in Nigeria; the process and dynamics of leadership; and technicalities of organizational design, development, and practice. A comprehensive literature search enabled a review of 130 journals and peer reviewed articles respectively, 19 books and 37 other sources including computer-generated libraries and internet links. A gap in the literature review revealed a lack of sufficient information available in the existing studies regarding how Nigerian citizens experience living through their governance system.

Chapter 3 described the responsibility of the researcher, as well as the research methodology, population, instrumentation, data collection process, and the development of data analysis. The chapter also provided substantial justification on why the qualitative method was the most appropriate for the current research study. Other elements in the chapter encompassed the study population, the sampling of participants, informed consent and confidentiality, internal and external validity, and reliability. Also discussed in the chapter was the interview process of data-collection which depended exclusively on lengthy interviews, through the use of open-ended and exploratory questions. Data analysis was performed with the seven-step Modified van Kaam Method (Moustakas, 1994). A detailed explanation of the role and process of obtaining informed consent from study participants were substantially explained. Other procedures explained in the chapter included, managing participants' confidentiality, study internal validity and external validity, and ethical considerations of the study practice.

In chapter 4, the study researcher explained the grouping, analysis, summary of the interview process, and the synthesizing of data according to the modified vann Kaam method (Moustakas, 1994). The chapter described with a detailed investigation, the process of data collection and analysis; identification of themes, and a summary of the findings. Also included in the chapter were the gathering of information obtained from the interviews, and how they were organized, coded and developed into themes for final assessment. Finally, the chapter presented a composite thematic textural-structural descriptions with an illustration of the lived experience of Nigerian citizens living through a political, cultural, social, and economic conditions. Findings in the research described moral philosophy, skills and training, effective management, and politics and diversity.

Findings

Findings developed by the current research study necessitates the most effective tools in organizational management. Some of the study findings also supported the discoveries in previous studies found in the current literature review for this research. The study findings and the implications validated the four common themes that emerged from the participants' responses. The responses resonated with all the participants regarding their experiences living under a governmental system facing political, economic, cultural and social challenges.

Theme 1: Moral Philosophy. Major findings in the current study included participants' experience of a culture of ethical lapses. Each participant expressed concerns about a high rate of bribery and corruption that infiltrated the system. The application of ethics in the management structure is an inevitable task for a leader who would inspire trust and transparency in the governance process (Bateman & Snell, 2007). Three branches of moral philosophy, namely Applied Ethics, Normative Ethics, and Analytic Ethics (Premeaux, 2009; Johnson, 2009; DeGeorge, 2010) are consistent with the findings in the current study. Applied Ethics entail day-to-day moral decisions, Normative Ethics emphasize on the application of those, whereas Analytic Ethics examines the choice and nature of morality. Collectively, the three ethical practices direct the fundamental demands of ethical values, and helps to determine the disparities between the right and wrong choices.

These discoveries in the current study are similar to the existing literature review findings of Schaubroeck, et al. (2012) emphasizing the positive implications of implanting ethical leadership within and across organization levels. Leadership and culture influence ethical understandings and behaviors of followers. The inspirations of ethical leadership occur directly among both immediate followers and across hierarchical ranks (Yukl, 2010; Jones, 2010). As one of the participants, SS-1, noted, "my state governor is not the one to tell me that it is wrong to demand money or bribe from a citizen to render him the service I am employed for." Thus, a system where ethical issues are reserved only for the citizens or the followers will dwindle in wide-range of corruption and process indecency.

Individuals remain the primary referent of the study of ethics and morality (DeGeorge, 2010). SS-1 expressed the role of citizens in promoting an ethical culture by comparing Nigeria to the United Stated where he visited. SS-1 said, "I have been here for just about a week and have observed that good behavior is not just for the leaders but for all and sundry." SS 1 expressed surprised that even at the airports, the supermarkets, and other public places, the staffs were very professional and well behaved. The participant also stated, "In my country, the airport workers demanded bribes even to check in my baggage at the airport." The current literature review of DeGeorge (2010); Preissle (2008), and Waskey, (2008) found that the concept of decency is consistent with the part of human philosophy concerned with proper comportment and righteous living. Furthermore, the biblical inferences and commandments on righteousness dovetail the basic ethical expectations of day-to-day business processes. These views coincide with Aristotle's exploration of morality, and highlights judgment, virtue, and character as three significant elements of human decency (DeGeorge (2010). Moral laws, social standards, business structures, and moral people are all interconnected in shaping societal moral uprightness. Virtue ethics reveals the ideals in a person; identifies the admirable qualities that form ethical demeanor, and helps others to acquire these values (Johnson, 2009).

All the 12 participants in the current study also expressed concerns about widespread corruption in the leadership system. Phrases and sentences were dominated by words such as dishonest, fraud, embezzlement, bad leaders, bribery, and corruption. These findings therefore revealed a system submersed with exploitation, and presided by dishonest leaders who catered only for their interests. Ethical challenges are inevitable in any management setting, especially with the conflicting characteristics of moral duty, rights, and justice in management. One of the participants, NE-1, stated that corruption is rampant in the country because the leaders are corrupt, stating that erasing corruption can only be effective if it starts from the top. The current literature review of DeGeorge (2010) found a high correlation between the practice of ethics and effective management. Ethics management impels organizational integrity, and this is determined by the role in promoting those expectations established, cultivated, and mandated by the leadership. Study findings showed a nonchalant attention accorded to deplorable matter of bribery, corruption, election-rigging, embezzlement and other types of violations borne out of lapses in moral values. A failure to strategically address the issues of ethics rendered the entire populace susceptible to corruption.

Ethical philosophy and organizational culture are inseparable (Wray-Bliss, 2011; Yukl, 2010; Jones, 2010). A current literature review of Wray-Bliss (2011) found that an organization must possess a code of ethics that governs tasks, services, and organizational behavior. In the public service environment where citizens receive various services, common ethical issues may arise from employee behavior, operational transparency, employee working conditions, technology management involving information, and individual privacies. This is because society consists of people with unique values, interests, feelings, and talents that may or may not be compatible with each other (Scott, 2007). Finding in the current study indicate that basic moral values are hardly observed in the Nigeria's public service systems. NE-1 talked about "kick-back" – a word used for bribery in the civil service. The implications was that government contractors usually spend enormous amount of money offering kickbacks to top government officials with little fund left to execute assigned contracts.

Current findings also indicate that citizens are unaware of any ethical codes in the public system. The discoveries were that citizens live in a system where bribery, corruption, and other moral desecrations are normal. This has undeniably hampered the practice of ethics in every segment of the society. It may be impracticable to achieve effective management without the controlling force of organizational culture of moral decency and civility. Azuka (2009) noted that without a commitment to fundamental values that direct the organization, the managing structure can deteriorate rapidly. Moral people are shaped by moral decency (DeGeorge, 2010). Adherence to ethical guidelines in making policies is one of the most significant machineries of governance prioritized in contemporary management (Yukl, 2010; Jones, 2010). Managing ethics and morality could therefore, require an organizational leadership and culture that impel fundamental models of ethical decision-making and action (Johnson, 2009).

Theme 2: Skills and Training. Findings from the current study highlighted lapses in managing skills in the public service system – a situation provoked by incompetence, inefficiency, a lack of adequate knowledge, and training. When the agents of governance are incompetent, tasks are hardly accomplished. Current study findings comprised the wraths of citizens shouldering the burden of incompetent leaders or managers. The current literature review also corroborated this phenomenon. Yukl (2013) found that one of the keys to an organization's long-term success lies in the skills of the leaders and their ability to rise up to impending challenges. This would entail developing a clear vision, supporting organizational structure of innovation, and committing to a strategic plan for performance accomplishment. Therefore, managing people and resources could entail leadership strategies that prioritize essential skills relevant to the task. Such skills could underscore transformational roles, such as vision, communication, mentoring, teamwork, goal setting, and accountability (Yukl, 2013; Nahavandi, 2012; Tichy & Devanna, 1990; Wren, 1995).

Leadership and training are inseparable themes. Research finding from a thread of interview data in this study reveal lapses in public education system – forcing citizens to seek education and working opportunities overseas. A study participant, SS-2 narrated how his son attends school in Ghana (a neighboring country) because he could not secure college admission in Nigeria. This discovery was consistent with the findings of Odunsi (1996) revealing that the lack of effective leadership in Nigeria has created extraordinary social problems unbearable to the citizens who now seek greener pastures in other countries. Quality education breeds innovative environment, quality of tasks, and development possibilities. Existing review findings of Shane (2011) noted that organizations are more innovative and successful in serving citizens' needs when leaders create respect for knowledge development and induct public servants to stay ahead of imminent challenges of management.

Findings in the current study indicate that most Nigerian past leaders lacked the necessary education relevant to their executive designations. This was aggravated by a string of military leaders who ruled without adequate training to govern people and resources. To corroborate this finding, one of the participants, SE-1 explained that a string of military officers without adequate training to govern the country provoked the prevailing hardship. A literary study of Bass (1990b) found that through training, leaders or managers can learn and acquire relevant transformational leadership qualities; such that enables them to inspire, energize, and intellectually stimulate subordinates. Finding by Bass was consistent with study conclusions of Kotter (2003) and Nahavandi (2012) specifying that the challenges of contemporary leadership is dependent on knowledge of the fundamental competencies. This would help leaders develop essential skills relevant to their specific tasks.

Theme 3: Ineffective Management. Findings in the current study showed that a lack of effective management of the political, economic, social, and cultural processes adversely impacted the lives of Nigerian citizens. This discovery was tied to the issues of unemployment, lack of amenities, lapses in basic development, and economic hardship which were frequently mentioned in participants' responses. All 12 participants blamed their leaders for not living up to their responsibilities and citizens' expectations. Study participant, SE-2 noted that family members as well as other struggling masses do not have access to basic live amenities such as; drinking water, good roads, and healthcare. The existing amenities may have also been neglected. SE-2 talked about how the only road leading to her village ruined vehicles and caused accidents and lives. SW-1 lost her niece while she was giving birth to her first child because she needed blood but there was none. These array of negative experiences by study participants is an indication that the system needed a transformation.

The existing literature review findings highlighted the role that leaders play in the transformation process. These findings were consistent with literature review findings of Burns (1978); Bass (1985); and Kuhn (1996). Studies by Burns (1978) and Bass (1985) of key contemporary leadership theories highlighted the significance of organizational transformation in effective management. The science of transformation in managing complex entities set the stage for modification of strategies, procedures, and processes to a proposed state. Another study by Kuhn (1996) found paradigm shift as a panacea for management transformation and organizational change.

Study further showed citizens yearning for effective leaders that can reward their patriotic spirits with basic amenities of life, such as good water, roads, electricity, schools, and other civic entitlements. This would encompass the pursuit of a new paradigm. The most fundamental stage of any management initiative in embracing a new paradigm is strategically to build a solid foundation for future developments. Paradigm shift, according to Kuhn is a change in thinking pattern, and not necessarily a workforce reshuffle (Avolio & Yammarino, 2002; Kuhn, 1996). It is a transformation process from the present to a projected future state of effective development (Jones, 2010). Findings from this study illuminates the positive impacts of transformational leadership on executive performance through the dynamic competencies of organizational learning and innovation. Studies have associated the transformational tenets with leadership development of skills. According to Bass (1990), transformational leadership can not only be learned, but also should be the focus in management training and development.

The current study found lack of adequate skills as contributory factors to Nigeria's leadership inadequacies. To reinvent leaders with necessary skills, change-oriented behavior could be prioritized to inspire innovation, shared learning, and the effective application of relevant organizational changes. Transformational leadership raises development capability and conveys upper levels of individual obligation among subordinates to organizational goals. These factors are facilitated through idealized influence, inspirational motivation, intellectual motivation, intellectual stimulation, and individualized consideration (Bass & Avolio, 1990). Leader with idealized influence can be trusted and respected. Inspirational motivation describes the ability to motivate and encourage team spirit. The ability to create and innovate through specific challenges defines the intellectual stimulation, whereas individualized consideration denotes an attitude towards coaching or encouraging subordinates to reach specific goals (Bass, 1990; Bass & Avolio, 1990).

There are links between organizational development (OD), organizational design, and managing people. The current research centers on people – the citizens of Nigeria living under a leadership condition immersed in political, cultural, social and economic complexities. Organizations are operated by people who make decisions. A leader plans, organizes, and controls the decision process. Studies by Jones (2010) and Huber (1986) found that the effectiveness and quality of these decisions determine the level of accomplishment of relevant tasks. This finding corroborates the current literature review findings of Jones (2004), Galbraith (2002), and Autry (1996). Jones (2004) found that leader rely on effective OD practice to mitigate challenging choices about the distribution of power, obligation, and accountability into units. These entail a coordination of responsibilities and motivation of the people who accomplish them. Autry (1996) indicated that leaders can apply the process of organizational design to coordinate people, tasks, and resources, and balance them with organizational purpose, vision, and strategy. Galbraith (2002) specified that organizations can rely on the framework for organizational design to make choices on operational structures. These policies provide essential tools for leaders to manage decisions and behaviors effectively in their organizations.

Theme 4: Politics and Diversity. Study findings in the current research included dichotomy among tribes and regions; a high level of tribalism in the public system, and reluctance of the leaders to develop the richness of Nigeria's culture to the benefit of its citizens. Existing studies have associated leadership effectiveness with issues of diversity management (Yukl, 2013; Nahavandi, 2012). As current literature review indicated, Nigeria is enriched with about 250 ethnic groups with different languages, beliefs, and religions. The challenged faced with managing this cluster of geographical zones; tribes and cultures were reflected in the study findings. The complexity of culture and managing people and resources pose inescapable challenges for managers because differences exist among individuals, populations, countries, and organizations (Yukl, 2013). An enduring theme that developed from the data in the current study were matters of cultural and tribal diversity, dominated by distressing issues of dichotomy in resources management. For example, one of the study participants, SS-1, noted, “I come from a region where we are mainly minorities, and we produce crude oil that sustains the entire country, but over the years, since independence, we have been marginalized and were excluded from sharing the national cake." The theme of politics, tribal, and cultural diversity is similar to the current review findings of the study conducted by Geert Hofstede (1980, 1993) on cross-cultural research on leadership (House, Wright, & Aditya, 1997). Hofstede's cross-cultural comparative study in the literature review suggests that familiarity could be developed with cultural resemblances and differences between and among leaders (Munley, Couto, & O'Neill, 2010).

All the participants blamed a prevalent discrimination in the public service to favoritism borne out of cultural and tribal affiliation. NC-2 noted that Nigeria’s multi-tribal culture have created more division than unity. In the existing literature, Hofstede's cross-cultural dimensions namely "power distance, uncertainty avoidance, individualism, masculinity, and long-term orientation" (Moskowitz, 2009, p. 3) are perceived as fundamental remedies to ethnic intricacies. For instance, three indexes, Power Distance, Masculinity and Femininity, and Uncertainty Avoidance are consistent with findings on issues of Nigeria's tribal and cultural differences. Power Distance Index measures how the less privileged recognize the fairness of power distribution. The index of Masculinity and Femininity discusses gender disparities. Uncertainty Avoidance measures the acceptance of uncertainty and ambiguity, and specifies how members of organizations are culturally programmed to express their feelings in unstructured circumstances.

Another approach to managing a multicultural entity was found in the review of existing literature of Tidd and Bessant (2011), specifying that effective leadership plan must encompass not only the systems, but also the people and the culture where they operate. Tasks are performed by human beings who have emotional and psychological needs. Expression of a vision has a negative effect on followers' confidence, unless accompanied by inspirational communication associated with commitment and interpersonal assistance with behaviors. This study is consistent with findings in the current study related to ethnic or tribal sentiments and dichotomy in the public system. One of the participants, SW-1, stated, "It is unfortunate that our cultures have divided us into tribes and religion. Right now, I do not trust my Muslim brothers because of too many killings in the north. This is how the cultural process is affecting my life as a citizen." Public servants tormented with these issues are not likely to render effective performance. Hence, the context of the effective management could instill into the system, flexible policies that accord respect for various cultures and ethnicities.

To substantiate current study findings on dichotomy and a high level of tribalism in the Nigeria's public service system, an existing literature review of Fasan (2002) found an interconnection between culture and politics. Organizational politics in Nigeria has triggered destructive resistance in the past. Further findings in the current study revealed the complex politics of resources management unfavorable to the general populace. The management of who gets what, where, when, and how are pervaded by tribal or zonal dichotomy that left many groups totally disenfranchised. As one of the participants, NC-2 noted, "If you rightly look at it, you would notice that every single regime including the present government is guilty of favoring one group or the other. It is a culture that has been there from the beginning."

Studies by Badham (2008); Brown (2011), and Harris and Kacmar (2005) found that the failure to properly integrate power and politics in management can destabilize power procedure among members and units. Nonetheless, leaders can encourage an organizational culture that circumscribes diversity and inspires inclusivity. Brown (2011) cautioned that voices of dissent to public policy program should not be interpreted as a rejection of the process. Allowing such opposing voices creates adequate opportunities to manage complaints and concerns. "It is also very possible that through negotiations and discussions, contributions of those being asked to change may improve the change program, and their participation may increase the likelihood of the changes being accepted," (Brown, 2011, p. 158).

Limitations

The purpose of this qualitative phenomenological research study was to understand how political, cultural, social and economic conditions in Nigeria influence the lives of Nigerian citizens through lived experiences of two citizens from each of the six geopolitical regions of the country namely, North-Central, North-Eastern, North-Western, South-Eastern, South-South, and South-Western regions. In research studies, limitations are used to detect potential study weaknesses (Simon, 2006). The major limitation encountered in the current study included the threat of inadequate data often prompted by the honesty of participants. The present of researcher, which is often mandatory in qualitative research, can affect participants' responses. This concern was mitigated through the Informed Consent clause explained in Appendix A. The document encouraged each of the participant to narrate their experiences in the most precise manner without fear of breach of confidentiality. Another limitation is that the study analysis and interpretation would have been time-consuming based on the voluminous nature of data in the qualitative process. To mitigate this shortfall and inspire process swiftness and accuracy, the current study used Nvivo 10® software to systematically code a large file of interview transcriptions.

Another limitation was that the study limited it sample collection from the six geopolitical regions of the country. The results may have been different if the study considered the lived experiences of citizens from each of the 36 states of Nigeria. Furthermore, sample selection in the current study did not consider the age ranks and gender of participants. Exploring how different age groups or gender experience living through political, cultural, social and economic conditions in Nigeria may offer an entirely different results and conclusions.

Implications

Findings from the current research study indicated the need for Nigeria to adopt a paradigm change through the application of moral philosophy, managerial competencies, change and transformation management, and effective management of politics and diversity. Study findings emerged from the themes. The first theme was related to issues of morality. Ethical philosophy and organizational culture are inseparable. Evidence presented by Schaubroeck, et al. (2012) substantiated the necessities of ethical leadership within and across all levels of organization. Leadership and culture influence ethical understandings and behaviors of citizens. Thus, the practice of moral decency is binding to both the leaders and the led. The second theme addressed findings associated with lapses in managing skills among the leadership. Studies by Yukl (2013) found that organization's long-term success is dependent on the skills of the leaders and their ability to rise up to impending challenges. The third theme was substantiated by Kuhn (1962), revealing paradigm shift as a panacea for transformation and change management. Findings in the current study revealed citizens' concerns of Nigeria's political, cultural, social and economic management. A paradigm shift thus remains a considerable option. Citing the study review of Tidd and Bessant (2011), the final theme, politics and diversity presented a substantiation that effective leadership plan must encompass not only the systems, but also the people and the culture where they operate. Effective management of diversity would reconcile overwhelming tribal concerns established by findings in the current study.

Whereas this study is about Nigerian citizens living through the system under investigation, consideration was accorded to the theoretical framework which focused on the theories of leadership. The findings supported the theory that there are fundamental connections between leadership styles, behavioral styles, and followership (Chaleff, 1995; Kellerman, 1984; Burns, 1978). Leading people entails managing their needs, resources, and environment. These substantially illustrated the theory that leadership and behavioral styles determine the quality of life of the citizens.

The current study aimed to answer the fundamental research question: How do Nigerian citizens describe their experience of living under economic, political, cultural, and social hardships? The research question was adequately answered as the data from all of the study participants showed the true reflections of citizens' experience under the phenomenon. Participants' experiences were organized into relevant themes namely; moral philosophy, skills and training, ineffective management, and politics, and diversity. These themes supported the study findings and recommendations. Findings and conclusions also revealed the burden of past and present challenges of managing a multi-tribal nation. These, coupled with the inability of the leaders to live up to their responsibilities accounted for the citizens' disparaging experience of the system. Recommendations of the study discussed in the next section offered effective leadership behavior and practices to improve the lives of Nigerian citizens.

Recommendations for Leaders

At one time, noted Mahatma Gandhi, an eminent civil rights leader of movement for the Indian independence, "leadership may have meant muscles, but today it means getting along with people" (Chew, 2011, p. 130). Thus, the charismatic portrait of the modern leadership looks nothing like Fidel Castro. It is a faceless portrait that epitomizes the toughness of Ronald Reagan, Nelson Mandela's charisma, and the most compassionate heart of Mother Theresa. The current study is about Nigerian citizens living through a political, economic, social, and cultural phenomena of leadership catastrophe. Hence, salvaging the situation requires effective leaders equipped with transformational competencies to manage not just the people, but also their environment, needs, civic responsibilities, entitlements, and other basic necessities.

As primary benefits, research studies enable individuals to make more informed decisions, develop work environments, and gain new knowledge (Moustakas, 1994). The result and conclusions of the current research findings created substantial recommendations for future leaders and future studies in management in organizational leadership. Findings comprised an understanding of Nigeria's management process through the live experience of citizens living through it. The study results uncovered fundamental leadership gaps in management, discussed the implications, and offered constructive mitigation strategies. Conclusions added new information to existing knowledge of leadership and the Nigerian management system. The recommendations for leaders focused primarily on the themes identified in the current study. Interconnections between these themes reflected the problem statement and study purpose, and corroborated the findings and recommendations. The recommendations are categorized as moral philosophy, organizational change, transformation, and diversity management. These remedies can help the present and aspiring leaders to develop effective leadership strategies to manage their citizens, public service system, and resources.

Moral Philosophy. In a research study where phrases of bribery and corruption overwhelm findings, application of moral philosophy in the Nigeria management structure remains a predictable task for building trust and transparency in governance. The first recommendation was that Nigerian leaders could embrace an all-encompassing organizational culture of ethics and moral decency. Three branches of moral philosophy were recommended: Applied Ethics entail the day-to-day moral decisions, Normative Ethics emphasize on the application, whereas Analytic Ethics examines the choice and nature of morality (Premeaux, 2009; Johnson, 2009; De-George, 2010). These three concept applications can help Nigerian leaders as well as other leaders to ask the fundamental questions of how to discover the disparities between right and wrong.

Johnson (2009) suggested that managing ethics and morality require an organizational leadership and culture that impel fundamental models of ethical decision-making and action. Moral decency shapes moral people. Organizational culture is developed by people, principles, and organizational structure. Therefore, it may be impracticable for the Nigerian leaders to embrace an ethical environment without the controlling force of organizational culture. Moral structure drives moral culture. Nigeria (both the leaders and the led) could note that ethics is not a constitutional duty, but moral obligations impelled by individual demeanor. It takes moral people to reinforce moral organizations because moral people create and sustain moral structures. As DeGeorge, (2010) noted, when structures and laws are immoral, people are encouraged to act immorally, and vice versa.

Based on findings in the current study about moral laxity in the Nigeria's system, implanting ethical philosophy in every facet of the decision-making process could be prioritized. Beyond individual considerations, Nigerian leaders could encourage an ethical environment by offering incentives for ethical behavior and applicable penalties to punish unethically practices. In furtherance of adherence to an environment devoid of social and executive decadence, organizations must go beyond conventional rules and encourage individuals on the roles of character and virtue in moral philosophy. Virtue ethics emphasizes the role of one's character and the qualities that it represents. Nigerian leaders through training and knowledge-sharing could inspire moral character by facilitating discussions on ethics, emphasizing conscientiousness, compassion, and responsibility rather than a traditional reliant on rules and government regulations.

Finally, recognizing the danger signs of ethical lapses can help leaders manage and maintain the ethical culture. As best practices in mitigating lapses, Bateman – Snell (2007) suggested some danger signs of what may be deemed as encouraging unethical behavior:

1. Lack of or ineffective code of ethics
2. Passion for short-term solutions to ethical issues
3. Consideration of ethics solely as a legal issue with the least consideration to individual character

4. Lack of explicit ethical procedures
5. Unwillingness of leaders to take ethical stands

Organizational Change. The second recommendation was that Nigerian leaders embrace an organizational change of the current management structure in the public service system. Managing change in this context is a quest targeted toward improving effectiveness at fundamental levels of the government for performance quality (Jones, 2011). To facilitate this challenge, leaders could initiate strategies to train employees on the implementation process. They could ensure that the projected goals are met and installed as part of the organizational culture. Paradigmatic change works best with an organization in crisis (Kuhn, 1996). As a fundamental revitalization tool, this process potentially renews the system with new values and innovative possibilities rather than the traditional standard practices.

To effectively make significant changes in its public sectors, Nigerian leaders could develop functioning plans to manage the transformation process. They could train all public employees on the change implementation methods to help mitigate process consequences. Other recommended strategies relevant to the change-management actions are explained as follows;

1. Change and Leadership: Dynamics of leadership effectiveness toward change could entail an exploration of contemporary management approach characterized by new ideas more receptive to competition, and very committed to the renewal process.

2. Change and Follower Involvement: In a multi-tribal country like Nigeria, citizens' involvement and commitment in a change process can be encouraged. Isolating citizens in any change process can provoke resistance and resentment.

3. Change and Interpersonal Relationship: Personal communication of the process reduces risks of resistance. Employees and citizens are human beings who have emotional and psychological needs. Expression of a vision could entail inspirational communication associated with commitment and interpersonal helping behaviors.

4. Change and Adequate Training: Training and knowledge development drive change and innovation possibilities. Public employees must be trained on the change implementation methods to impel success and help mitigate process consequences.

5. Change and Managing Failure: Innovation management entails the ability to articulate the realities of failure. To be more innovative, leaders could embrace an organizational culture that tolerates failure as a transformation challenge rather than a disgrace. As Shane (2009) indicated, people will not try to do new things if they know that they will be punished or degraded if they fail.

Transformation. The third recommendation was that leaders embrace a comprehensive transformation agenda to overhaul the leadership system. A correlation of leadership theories, styles, and behaviors supported the framework for the current qualitative phenomenological study. Study by Wren (1995) ascribed leadership to the constant interaction of three essential elements: the leaders, the followers, and the surrounding situation. Based on the above evidence, a combination of applicable components of transactional and transformational management strategies was recommended. This would inspire a leader-follower relations where both parties engage themselves to greater heights of motivation and morality (Bass & Avolio, 1994). To facilitate this measure, leaders could integrate fundamental behaviors of contemporary leadership practice associated with tasks, behavior, change, participation, and transformation.

In this modern era of organizational transformation, a leader must be prepared to be prudent risk-taker who directs risky and innovative solutions involving unexpected outcomes. Such a leader could inspire change, motivate subordinates, and carry them along toward the finishing line (Kotter (2012). In Nigerian, a system still tormented by the wraths of past military dictatorship (History, 2008; Rotimi & Ihonvbere, 1994; Joseph, 2012), a transformational approach was recommended as an inevitable remedy. The leaders must be trusted and respected. Finally, this leader should be equipped with relevant skills to connect with others, develops shared directions, create a secure environment, and allow flexibility for change and innovation.

As a part of transformation management, leaders and managers could evaluate and measure performance at all public service sectors. This would entail establishing a process to regulate and improve the transformation process at three performance levels — organization, process, and the workforce (Rummler & Brache, 2013). Transformation process without performance evaluation might be unreasonable. In a system where lapses in leadership have negatively influenced citizens, an effective change initiative could corroborate performance and feedback. Rummler and Brache (2013) warned that driving a transformation project to its final stage is not the end; it is just the beginning. Hence, effective machinery could be established in both the leadership and the public service system to evaluate performance consistently, or the transformation process would fail.

The most fundamental need of performance evaluation and measurement is that it helps leaders or managers think and behave in new ways toward service perfection. Furthermore, it promotes competence and instills trust and accuracy in the system. Leaders could, therefore, prioritize the task evaluation of the people, process, and performance to expedite a transition from strategic transformational vision to organizational reality. To effectively facilitate these standards, managers, as a recommendation, could establish appropriate measures and goals to track or identify actual performance. They could record the contrasting gaps in measurement, and use the figures as the basis for decision-making and performance perfection.

Managing politics and multiculturalism. Managing diversity in Nigeria has become a matter of significance provoked by multiplicity of tribes and cultures. Leaders are currently confronted with the increasing need to manage people from a cluster of cultures and tribes, and could therefore, understand the structure of multicultural management. The fourth and final recommendation was that Nigerian leaders coordinate and integrate disparities in their tribes, tongue, and cultures with formal laws and legislation. Using the United States as an example, one of the participants, SE-2, echoed a similar sentiment suggesting effective policies to accommodate all ethnicities. Findings in this study are a justification of the disparaging implications of disenfranchising any demographic sector from their civic entitlements. As fundamental remedy, an existing study by Guchteneire (2007) found that constitutional arrangements could serve as a mediation tool between or among different groups. This would entail their shared privileges of independence, citizen's rights to participate in the governance process, and objective distribution of power and resources. To facilitate these measures, Geert Hofstede's cross-cultural comparative study research on leadership was recommended. Indexes such as Power Distance, Masculinity and Femininity, and Uncertainty Avoidance discussed in Chapter 2, were consistent with study findings and can mitigate issues of tribal and cultural differences.

Study findings also show that Nigeria's measure of diversity were basically limited to tribes, religion, and geographical origins. Studies by DeGeorge, (2010); Yukl (2013), and Nahavandi (2012) found that classes of diversity could be expanded to reflect all demographic groups. As a major recommendation, leaders could diversify recognition and management of cultural multiplicity at other capacities, especially in women and minority affairs. Five selection criteria were recommended;

1. ***Corporate Diversity:*** Commitment to diversity through corporate initiatives.
2. ***Community Diversity:*** Special recognition and encouragement of a culture of community service, philanthropy and education development.
3. ***Gender Diversity:*** Promoting gender diversity with gender equality, education, and leadership development.
4. ***Cross-Cultural Diversity:*** Leaders must encourage and promote issues of cross-cultural diversity to create a rapport among tribes and cultures.

5. ***Leadership Diversity:*** encouraging leadership effectiveness to reflect gender, tribe, age, race, and individuality.

Recommendations for Future Research

The current research study explored how political, cultural, social and economic conditions in Nigeria influence the lives of Nigerian citizens through lived experiences of two citizens from each of the six geopolitical regions of the country. This research centered on people (Nigerian citizens), through the subjects of management and leadership, and through the processes of managing and leading. Based on the findings, opportunities do exist for further studies in the area of leadership, managing people and resources. Future researchers can replicate this study by using qualitative phenomenological study to explore the experiences of citizens in other countries living through similar challenges. Future phenomenological studies could also focus on other African countries where citizens experience inadequacies in people and resources management. This could help leaders in such regions to direct constructive performance intervention of startling governance anguishes.

Other research opportunities could be explored with a different theoretical framework to create from a different perspective, an understanding of how other conditions influence the lives of Nigerian citizens. Furthermore, the current qualitative study drew samples from two citizens from each of the six geopolitical regions of the country. Conducting a qualitative study with samples from the 36 states of Nigeria might offer a new set of resources and geographical enlargement. Unlike the current study, future research may expand demographic categories to age and gender. For example, exploring how different age or gender groups experience living through a leadership condition in Nigeria may offer an entirely different dimension to the study of Nigeria's leadership.

Whereas the scope of this research was limited specifically to Nigerian citizens now living under the leadership system, the data in the current research involve other factors that can lead to future studies. For instance, as stated in the problem statement, bad leadership has cost the Nigerian government the migration to foreign countries, an exceptionally skilled manpower made up of talented professionals who are saddened by insufficient economic rewards and unfavorable work condition. Future qualitative studies may be conducted on Nigerian citizens in the diaspora about a comparison of their experiences in the Nigerian system and their current countries of residence. This dimension might generate yet other relevant conclusions that can empower future leaders with effective tools and strategies in managing people and resources to encourage retention and reduce brain drain.

Summary

The current research study focused on the Nigerian citizens and their living through an influence of political, cultural, social, and economic conditions. Chapter 5 provided a summary of four proceeding chapters. The chapter also offered detailed discussions about the significance of the study, the implications and conclusions. Substantial recommendations for future research studies pertaining to study of management in organizational leadership were adequately presented. Findings through a systematic analysis of citizens' experience revealed an insightful understanding of Nigeria's management process, unveiling the lapses, analyzing the implications, and creating constructive mitigation strategies. Conclusions added new information to existing knowledge of management in organizational leadership and the development of effective leaders in managing people, their needs, and resources. The qualitative study helped to explore the fundamental research question: How do Nigerian citizens describe their experience of living under economic, political, cultural, and social hardships?

The chapter provided recommendations for Nigerian leaders and future researchers. As shown in Figure 7, recommendations for leaders and managers corroborated through study findings related to leadership and management were generated from four emerging themes. The themes identified were moral philosophy, skills and training, ineffective management, and politics and diversity. The first common theme on ethics considered the application of moral philosophy in the management structure as an inevitable task for effective management. Moral philosophy was recommended. The second theme on skills emerged from concerns about inefficiency. The theme analyzed leadership skills and training as recommendations. The third theme on effective management emerged from concerns about lack of amenities. The theme found paradigm shift as a panacea for managing transformation and organizational change. Transformation was recommended. The fourth theme on organizational politics and diversity emerged from concerns about dichotomy and tribalism. The theme corroborated leadership effectiveness with issues of politics and managing tribes, cultures, and zones. Diversity management was recommended. Limitations and recommendations of the study were also discussed. Future studies were recommended to replicate the current study in other geographical locations, especially in countries where citizens are living through similar challenges.

Figure 7

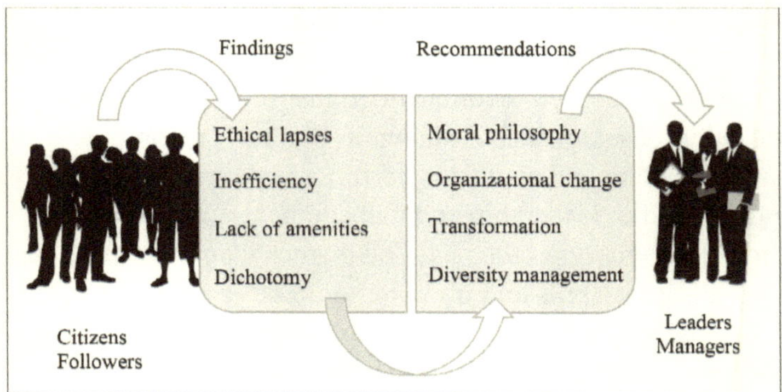

Figure 7. A flow chart showing summary of complete study findings and recommendations.

The findings emerged from comprehensive themes that supported the study conclusions.

Note. From the researcher, based on study findings and recommendations.

References

Achebe, C. (1983). *The Trouble with Nigeria.* Oxford: Heinemann Publishers.

Abawi, L. (2012). Introducing refractive phenomenology. International *Journal of Multiple Research Approaches, 6*(2), 141-149.

Abdullahi, H., Yahya, Z. A., & Yelwa, M. (2012). Corruption in Nigeria: towards a new paradigm for effective democratic governance and sustainable development. *Academic Research International, 3*(1), 239-253. Retrieved from http://search.proquest.com/docview/1266030367?accountid=35812

Adams, C., & Manen, M. (2008). Phenomenology. In L. Given (Ed.), *The SAGE encyclopedia of qualitative research methods.* (pp. 615-620). Thousand Oaks, CA: SAGE Publications, Inc. doi: http://dx.doi.org.ezproxy.apollolibrary.com/10.4135/9781412963909.n317

Adegboye, M. (2013). The applicability of management theories in Nigeria: Exploring the cultural challenge. *International Journal of Business and Social Science, 4*(10) Retrieved from http://search.proquest.com/docview/1437608957?accountid=35812

Agbiboa, D. E. (2012). Between corruption and development: The political economy of state robbery in Nigeria. *Journal of Business Ethics, 108*(3), 325-345. doi:http://dx.doi.org/10.1007/s10551-011-1093-5

Ajayi, G. (2007). T*he military and the Nigerian state, 1966-1993: a study of the strategies of political power control.* Africa World Press, Trenton New Jersey, ISBN 1-59221-568-8

American Psychological Association (2002). Ethical principles of psychologists and code of conduct. *American Psychologist, 57*(12).

Anthony, S., & Jack, S. (2009). Qualitative case study methodology in nursing research: an integrative review. *Journal of Advanced Nursing, 65*(6), 1171-1181. doi:10.1111/j.1365-2648.2009.04998. Retrieved from http://web.ebscohost.com.ezproxy.apollolibrary.com/ehost/pdfviewer/pdfviewer?vid=3&hid=15&sid=dd66edbb-2e32-4880-90cd-46fdf2107276%40sessionmgr10

Azuka, E. B. (2009). Ethics of leadership and the integrity question among leaders. *Ife Psychology, 17*(1), 11-26. Retrieved from http://search.proquest.com/docview/219469248?accountid=35812

Avolio J. B., Gardner L. W. (2005). Authentic leadership development: Getting to the root cause of positive forms of leadership. *Leadership Quarterly, 16,* 315-338.

Babbie, E. (2001). *The practice of social research* (9th ed.). Belmont, CA: Wadsworth Thomson Learning.

Background Notes on Countries of the World: *Nigeria, 1.*

Badham, R. (2008). Organizational politics. In S. Clegg, & J. Bailey (Eds.), *International encyclopedia of organization studies.* (pp. 1157-1161). Thousand Oaks, CA: SAGE Publications, Inc. doi: http://dx.doi.org.ezproxy.apollolibrary.com/10.4135/9781412956246.n394

Bailey, C.A. (1996). *A guide to field research.* Thousand Oaks, CA: Pine Forge.

Ballinger, C. (2008). Accountability. In L. Given (Ed.), *The SAGE encyclopedia of qualitative research methods.* (pp. 4-5). Thousand Oaks, CA: SAGE Publications, Inc. doi: http://dx.doi.org.ezproxy.apollolibrary.com/10.4135/9781412963909.n3

Bass & Bass (2008). T*he Bass Handbook of Leadership: Theory, Research, and Managerial Applications"* 4th edition Free Press

Bass, B. M., and Avolio, B. J. (1994). *Improving organizational effectiveness through transformational leadership.* Thousand Oaks, CA: Sage Publications.

Bass, B. M. (1990). *Bass and Stogdill's handbook of leadership.* New York: Free Press.

Bass, B. M. & Avolio, B. J. (1990). Transformational leadership development: Manual for the Multifactor. *Leadership Questionnaire.* Palo Alto, CA: Consulting Psychologist Press

Bassett, B. (2010). Computer-based analysis of qualitative data: NVIVO. In A. Mills, G. Durepos, & E. Wiebe (Eds.), *Encyclopedia of case study research.* (pp. 193-195). Thousand Oaks, CA: SAGE Publications, Inc. doi: http://dx.doi.org.ezproxy.apollolibrary.com/10.4135/9781412957397.n71

Bateman, T. S., & Snell, S. A. (2007). *Management: Leading and collaborating in a competitive world* (7th Ed.). Boston, MA: McGraw-Hill/Irwin.

Beagrie, S. (2004). How to conduct a SWOT analysis. *Personnel Today, 21.* Retrieved from http://search.proquest.com/docview/229950392?accountid=35812

Benjamin, S. A. (1999). The 1996 state and local government reorganizations in Nigeria. *Nigerian Institute of Social and Economic Research, Ibadan, Nigeria,* ISBN 978-181-238-9

Besio, K. (2010). The politics and ethics of trust in geographic research. In S. Smith, R. Pain, S. Marston, & J. Jones (Eds.). *The Sage Handbook of Social Geographies.* (pp. 560-573). London: SAGE Publications Ltd. doi: http://dx.doi.org.ezproxy.apollolibrary.com/10.4135/9780857021113.n26

Bhal, K., & Leekha, N. (2008). Exploring cognitive moral logics using grounded theory: the case of software piracy. *Journal of Business Ethics, 81*(3), 635-646. Doi: 10.1007/s10551-007-9537-7

Blackshaw, T. (2009). Ethics. *In The sage dictionary of leisure studies.* (pp. 71-72). London: SAGE Publications Ltd. doi: http://dx.doi.org.ezproxy.apollolibrary.com/10.4135/9781446213278.n77

Boote, D. N., & Beile, P. (2005). Scholars before researchers: On the centrality of the dissertation literature review in research preparation. *Educational Researcher, 34*(6), 3-15. doi:10.3102/0013189X034006003

Bolden, R., Gosling, J., Marturano, A. and Dennison, P (2006). A review of leadership theory and Competency Frameworks. *Centre for Leadership Studies University of Exeter, United Kingdom.* Retrieved from http://centres.exeter.ac.uk/cls/documents/mgmt_standards.pdf

Brown, D. R. (2011). *An experiential approach to organization development* (8th ed.). Boston, MA: Prentice Hall.

Burns, J. A. (1995). Transactional and Transformational Leadership. In J.T. Wren (ed.), *The leader's companion: Insights into leadership through the ages.* New York: The Free Press. [Reprinted courtesy of the *Journal of Contemporary Business, 3*(Autumn1974) published by the School of Business Administration, University of Washington, Seattle, WA.

Burns, J. M. (1978). *Leadership.* New York: Harper & Row

Campbell, I. (2009). Coup d'état. In *The Concise Oxford Dictionary of Politics.* : Oxford University Press. Retrieved 13 Oct. 2013, from http://www.oxfordreference.com/view/10.1093/acref/9780199207800.001.0001/acref-9780199207800-e-295.

Caux Round Table (2013). Vision, Mission, Purpose. Retrieved from http://www.cauxroundtable.org/index.cfm?&menuid=142

Chemers, M. M. (1995). Contemporary leadership theories. In J.T. Wren (ed.), *The leader's companion: Insights on leadership through the ages.* New York: The Free Press. [Reprinted courtesy of the *Journal of Contemporary Business, 3*(1974).]

Chew, M. (2011). Discover your leadership style. Singapore: Armour Publishing Ltd.

Christensen, L. B., Johnson, R. B., & Turner, L. A. (2010, 2011). *Research Methods, Design, and Analysis* (11ed.). Boston, MA: Allyn & Bacon.

Chukwuemeka, O., & Ntunde, F. O. (2011). Eradication of poverty and hunger in Nigeria: Issues and options for attainment of millennium development goals. *Canadian Social Science, 7*(6), 109-113. doi:10.3968/j.css.1923669720110706.420

Clawson J.G. (2006). *Level Three Leadership: Getting Below the Surface*, Third Edition, Published by Pearson Prentice Hall. Copyright © 2006 by Pearson Education, Inc.

Coawin R. G. (1972). Strategies for organizational innovation: an empirical comparison A*merican Sociological Review 1972, Vol. 37* (August):441-454 (EBSCOHOST).

Cohen, M. Z., Kahn, D. L., & Steeves, R. H. (2000). *Hermeneutic phenomenological research: A practical guide for nurse researchers.* Thousand Oaks, CA: Sage Publications.

Cone, J. D., & Foster, S. L. (2006). *Dissertations and theses from start-to finish* (2nd ed.), Washington, DC: American Psychological Association.

Craig, E (2002). Egoism. Excerpts from Richard Kraut's entry on Egoism in the *Routledge Encyclopedia of Philosophy Version 1.0*, London: Routledge. Retrieved from http://www.phil.cmu.edu/cavalier/80130/part2/Routledge/R_Egoism.html

Cuilla J. (1998). *Ethics, the heart of leadership.* Westport, CT: Quorum Books.

Daniels, Gilda, (2010). Expand the Racial Categories for Classification. *Insights on Law & Society*, 15312461, Winter 2010, Vol. 10, Issue 2.

Denzin, N. K., & Lincoln, Y. S. (Eds.). (1994). *Handbook of qualitative research.* Thousand Oaks, CA: Sage.

de Kluyver, C. A., & Pearce ll, J. A. (2012). *Strategy: A view from the top* (4th ed.). Upper Saddle River, NJ: Pearson.

DeGeorge, R. T. (2010). *Business ethics* (7th Ed.). Upper Saddle River, NJ: Prentice Hall.

Dreyfus, H. L., ed., & Wrathall, M. A., ed. (2006). *A companion to phenomenology and existentialism.* Oxford, UK: Blackwell.

Ebegbulem, J. C. (2012). Corruption and leadership crisis in Africa: Nigeria in focus. International *Journal of Business and Social Science, 3*(11), n/a. Retrieved from http://search.proquest.com/docview/1017542769?accountid=35812

Economy. (2009). In L. Sullivan (Ed.), *The SAGE glossary of the social and behavioral sciences.* (p. 169). Thousand Oaks, CA: SAGE Publications, Inc. doi: http://dx.doi.org.ezproxy.apollolibrary.com/10.4135/9781412972024.n831

Ezimma Kate, N. N. (2010). Defining and enforcing ethical leadership in Nigeria. African *Journal of Economic and Management Studies, 1*(1), 25-41. doi:http://dx.doi.org/10.1108/20400701011028149

Fasan, R. (2002). Politics, political culture, and socialization: Reinventing the Nigerian polity. *Journal of Cultural Studies, 4*(1), 156-184. Retrieved from http://search.proquest.com/docview/872163679?accountid=35812

Finlay, L. (2009). Debating phenomenological research. *Phenomenology & Practice, 3*(1), 6-25.

Fiedler, Fred E. (1967). *A theory of leadership effectiveness.* McGraw-Hill: Harper and Row Publishers Inc.

Flood, A. (2010). Understanding phenomenology. *Nurse Researcher, 17*(2), 7-15.

Frank, E. O., (2009). Accountability of government through the budget process: A paradigm shift. *Interdisciplinary Journal of Contemporary Research in Business, 1*(2), 38-50. Retrieved from http://search.proquest.com/docview/520188409?accountid=35812

Gallos, J.V. (2006, 2007). *Organization development.* A Francisco, CA; Jossey-Bass.

Gardner, J. W. (1995). The cry for leadership. In J.T. Wren (ed.), The leader's companion: Insights on *leadership through the ages.* New York: The Free Press. [Reprinted courtesy of the *Journal of Contemporary Business, Government and Political Conditions.*]

Glaser, BG. & Strauss, AL. (1967). *The discovery of grounded theory: Strategies for qualitative research.* New York: Aldine De Gruyter.

Grais, R. F., Dubray, C. C., Gerstl, S. S., Guthmann, J. P., Djibo, A. A., Nargaye, K. D., & ... Guerin, P. J. (2007). Unacceptably high mortality related to measles epidemics in Niger, Nigeria, and Chad. *Plos Medicine, 4*(1), 122-129. doi:10.1371/journal.pmed.0040016

Groenewald, T. (2004). A phenomenological research design illustrated. *International Journal of Qualitative Methods, 3*(1). Retrieved from http://www.ualberta.ca/~iiqm/backissues/3_1/pdf/groenewald.pdf

Halloran, M. (2007). Culture. In R. Baumeister, & K. Vohs (Eds.), *Encyclopedia of social psychology.* (pp. 211-213). Thousand Oaks, CA: SAGE Publications, Inc. doi: http://dx.doi.org.ezproxy.apollolibrary.com/10.4135/9781412956253.n127

Hammersley, M. (2004). Phenomenology. In M. Lewis-Beck, A. Bryman, & T. Liao (Eds.), *Encyclopedia of Social Science Research Methods.* (pp. 816-817). Thousand Oaks, CA: SAGE Publications, Inc. doi: http://dx.doi.org.ezproxy.apollolibrary.com/10.4135/9781412950589.n708

Hamilton, D. (2005). Phenomenology. In S. Mathison (Ed.), *Encyclopedia of evaluation.* (p. 315). Thousand Oaks, CA: SAGE Publications, Inc. doi: http://dx.doi.org.ezproxy.apollolibrary.com/10.4135/9781412950558.n416

Harris, K., & Kacmar, K. (2005). Organizational politics. In J. Barling, E. Kelloway, & M. Frone (Eds.), *Handbook of work stress.* (pp. 353-375). Thousand Oaks, CA: SAGE Publications, Inc. doi: http://dx.doi.org.ezproxy.apollolibrary.com/10.4135/9781412975995.n14

Heifetz, Ronald (1994). *Leadership without Easy Answers.* Cambridge, MA: Harvard University Press. ISBN 0-674-51858-6.

History. (2011). Background Notes on Countries of the World: *Nigeria, 5.*

History. (2011). Background Notes on Countries of the World: *Nigeria, 4.*

Hofstede, G. (1980). *Culture's consequences: International differences in work-related values*. London: Sage.

Hofstede, G. (1993). Cultural constraints in management theories. *Academy of Management Executive, 7,* 81–90.

Holstein, J. A., & Gubrium, J. F. (1994). Phenomenology, ethnomethodology, and interpretive practice. In N. K. Denzin & Y. S. Lincoln (Eds.), *Handbook of Qualitative Research* (pp. 262-272). Thousand Oaks, CA: Sage

Husserl, E. (1965). *Phenomenology and the crisis of philosophy: Philosophy as rigorous science and philosophy and the crisis of European man.* New York: Harper & Row.

Hycner, R. H. (1999). Some guidelines for the phenomenological analysis of interview data. In A. Bryman & R . . . G. Burgess (Eds.), *Qualitative research* (Vol. 3, pp. 143-164). London: Sage.

Idris, M. (2013). Corruption and insecurity in Nigeria. *Public Administration Research, 2*(1), 59-66. Retrieved from http://search.proquest .com/docview/1439818060?accountid=458

International Monetary Fund December (2005) Nigeria: Poverty Reduction Strategy Paper—*National Economic Empowerment and Development Strategy IMF Country Report No. 05*/433

Jencik, A. (2011). Qualitative versus quantitative research. In J. Ishiyama, & M. Breuning (Eds.), *21st century political science: A reference handbook.* (pp. 506-514). Thousand Oaks, CA: SAGE Publications, Inc. doi: http://dx.doi.org.ezproxy.apollolibrary.com/10.4135/9781412979351.n60

Johnson, C. E. (Ed.). (2009). *Meeting the ethical challenges of leadership: Casting light or shadow* (3rd Ed). Thousand Oaks, CA: Sage.

Jones, G.R. (2010). *Organizational theory, design, and change* (6th Ed.). Upper Saddle River, NJ: Prentice Hall.

Joseph, C. E. (2012). Corruption and leadership crisis in Africa: Nigeria in focus. *International Journal of Business and Social Science, 3*(11), n/a. Retrieved from http://search.proquest.com/docview/1017542769?accountid=35812

Kalaian, S., & Kasim, R. (2008). External validity. In P. Lavrakas (Ed.), *Encyclopedia of survey research methods.* (pp. 255-258). Thousand Oaks, CA: SAGE Publications, Inc. doi: http://dx.doi.org.ezproxy.apollolibrary.com/10.4135/9781412963947.n172

Kehinde, A. B. (2009). The culture of violence and the scramble for political power in Oyo state, Nigeria (1999-2006). *Ife Psychologies, 17*(1), 176-193. Retrieved from http://search.proquest.com/docview/219587682?accountid=35812

Knight Matthew (2011) Leadership secrets from the ancients. *The CNN.* Retrieved from http://edition.cnn.com/2011/BUSINESS/02/18/ancient.leadership.lessons/index.html

Koenig, M & de Guchteneire, P. (2007). Political governance of cultural diversity. *Democracy and Human Rights in Multicultural Societies.* Retrieved from http://www.ashgate.com/pdf/SamplePages/Democracy_and_Human_Rights_in_Multicultural_Societies_Intro.pdf

Krippendorff, K. H. (2013). *Content analysis: An introduction to its methodology* (3rd Ed.). SAGE Publications, Inc. Washington, DC.

Krupp, T. (2010). Phenomenology. In M. Bevir (Ed.), **Encyclopedia of political theory.** (pp. 1033-1037). Thousand Oaks, CA: SAGE Publications, Inc. doi: http://dx.doi.org.ezproxy.apollolibrary.com/10.4135/9781412958660.n338

Kuhlke, O. (2006). Culture. In B. Warf (Ed.), *Encyclopedia of human geography.* (pp. 81-83). Thousand Oaks, CA: SAGE Publications, Inc. doi: http://dx.doi.org.ezproxy.apollolibrary.com/10.4135/9781412952422.n57

Kuhn, T. (1996). *The structure of scientific revolutions.* Chicago, IL: The University of Chicago Press.

Kvale, S. (1996). *Interviews: An introduction to qualitative research interviewing.* Thousand Oaks, Calif: Sage Publications.

Lawal, T., Imokhuede, K., & Johnson, I. (2012). Governance crisis and the crisis of leadership in Nigeria. *International Journal of Academic Research in Business and Social Sciences, 2*(7), 185-191. Retrieved from http://search.proquest.com/docview/1437617839?accountid=458

Lincoln, Y. S., & Guba, E. G. (1985). *Naturalistic inquiry.* Newbury Park, California: Sage Publications Inc.

Machiavelli, N., Pospisil, L., Churchill, W., & von Heyking, J. (2004). Politics. In G. Goethals, G. Sorenson, & J. Burns (Eds.), *Encyclopedia of leadership.* (pp. 1210-1219). Thousand Oaks, CA: SAGE Publications, Inc. doi: http://dx.doi.org.ezproxy.apollolibrary.com/10.4135/9781412952392.n279

Madueke, C. N. (2008). The role of leadership in governance: The Nigerian experience. (Order No. 3320296, Walden University). *ProQuest Dissertations and Theses, 194*-n/a. Retrieved from http://search.proquest.com/docview/304414078?accountid=35812. (304414078).

Manen, M. (1997). *Researching lived experience: Human science for an action sensitive pedagogy.* Albany: State University of New York Press.

Mapp, T. (2008). Understanding phenomenology: the lived experience. B*ritish Journal of Midwifery, 16*(5), 308-311.

Merriam, S. B. (2009). *Qualitative research: A guide to design and implementation.* San Francisco, CA: Jossey-Bass.

Marshall, M. (1996). Sampling for qualitative research. *Family Practice, 13*(6), 522-525.

Martino, D. (2010). Phenomenology. In R. Jackson, & M. Hogg (Eds.), *Encyclopedia of identity.* (pp. 553-556). Thousand Oaks, CA: SAGE Publications, Inc. doi: http://dx.doi.org.ezproxy.apollolibrary.com/10.4135/9781412979306.n179

Maxwell, J. 2009. "Designing a qualitative study" in The Sate *Handbook for Applied Social Science Research* edited by L. Bickmam and D. Rog. Thousand Oaks, CA: Sage p. 222.

Maxwell, J. A. (2005). *Qualitative research design: An interactive approach. Applied social research methods series, v. 41.* Thousand Oaks, CA: Sage Publications.

McAuley, J., Duberley, J. & Johnson, P. (2007).*Organization theory: Challenges and perspectives.* Upper Saddle River, NJ: Prentice Hall.

Mercy, O. A. (2012). Civil society and democratic consolidation in Nigeria. *Journal of Emerging Trends in Educational Research and Policy Studies, 3*(1), 61-67. Retrieved from http://search.proquest.com/docview/1438289257?accountid=458.

Merriam, S. B. (2009). Qualitative research: A guide to design and implementation. San Francisco, CA: Jossey-Bass.

Miah, M. (2008). Social Development. *In Encyclopedia of Social Work.:* Oxford University Press. Retrieved 24 Oct. 2013, from http://www.oxfordreference.com/view/10.1093/acref/9780195306613.001.0001/acref-9780195306613-e-362.

Minkov, M., & Hofstede, G. (2011). The evolution of Hofstede's doctrine. *Cross Cultural Management, 18*(1), 10-20. doi:http://dx.doi.org/10.1108/13527601111104269

Miles, M. B., & Huberman, A. M. (1994). *Qualitative data analysis: An expanded sourcebook* (2nd ed.). Thousand Oaks, CA: Sage.

Moran, D. (2000). *Introduction to phenomenology.* London: Routledge.

Moustakas, C. (1994). *Phenomenological research methods.* Thousand Oaks, CA: Sage

Moskowitz, S. (2009). Hofstede's five dimensions of culture. In C. Wankel (Ed.), *Encyclopedia of business in today's world.* (pp. 817-819). Thousand Oaks, CA. SAGE Publications, Inc. doi: http://dx.doi.org.ezproxy.apollolibrary.com/10.4135/9781412964289.n468

Moseley, J. L., & Dessinger, J. C. (Eds.). (2010). *Handbook of improving performance in the workplace: Vol. 3.* Measurement and evaluation. San Francisco, CA: Pfeiffer.

Munley, A., Couto, R., & O'Neill, K. (2010). Leadership cultures. In R. Couto (Ed.), *Political and civic leadership: A reference handbook.* (pp. 498-505). Thousand Oaks, CA: SAGE Publications, Inc. doi: http://dx.doi.org.ezproxy.apollolibrary.com/10.4135/9781412979337.n56

Nadler, David A. and Tushman Michael L. (1995). Beyond the charismatic leader: leadership and organizational change. In *J.T. Wren (ed.), The leader's companion: Insights on leadership through the ages.* New York: The Free Press. [Reprinted courtesy of the *Journal of Contemporary Business, 3*(Autumn 1974).

Nahavandi, A. (2006). *The art and science of leadership.* (4th Ed.). Upper Saddle River, NJ: Pearson.

Neumann, W. L. (2005). *Social research methods: Qualitative and quantitative approaches* (6th Ed.). Boston, MA: Allyn & Bacon.

"Nigeria." CultureGrams Online Edition. *ProQuest, 2013.* Web. 21 Oct 2013.

Nigeria economy: Poverty levels rise. (2012). New York: *The Economist Intelligence Unit*. Retrieved from http://search.proquest.com/docview/962411584?accountid=35812

Nigeria (2011). Political Risk Yearbook: *Nigeria Country Report,* PRI-1-20.

Nigeria profile (2013). A chronology of key events. *BBC News Africa.* Retrieved from http://www.bbc.com/news/world-africa-13951696

Niworu, S. M. (2013). Boko Haram sect: Terrorists or a manifestation of the failed Nigerian state. *Journal of Politics and Law, 6*(2), 245-250. Retrieved from http://search.proquest.com/docview/1439254864?accountid=458

Odion, S., & Omolere, M. (2011). Nigeria and the challenges of credible political leadership since 1960. *Canadian Social Science, 7*(4), 136-143. doi:10.3968/j.css.1923669720110704.035

Odunsi B. (1996). An analysis of brain-drain and its impact on manpower development in Nigeria. *Journal of Third World Studies. Spring 96 1996; 13*(1):193-214.

Odunsi B. (1996). The impact of leadership instability on democratic process in Nigeria. *Journal of Asian & African Studies, 31*(1/2):66.

Ogunbadejo, Oye (1979) Conflict Images: Colonial' Legacy, Ethnicity, and Corruption in Nigerian Politics, 1960-1966. *Utafiti-Vol.4* No.1 July 1979. Retrieved from http://archive.lib.msu.edu/DMC/African%20Journals/pdfs/Utafiti/vol4no1/aejp004001009.pdf

Ogundele, O. J. K., P., & Hassan, A. R., P. (2011). Challenges of ethics in Nigeria within the context of global ethical practice. Interdisciplinary *Journal of Contemporary Research in Business, 3*(7), 510-528. Retrieved from http://search.proquest.com/docview/923787224?accountid=35812

Ojo, O. D., Ugochukwu, N. O. A., & Obinna, E. J. (2011). Understanding the escalation of brain drain in Nigeria from poor leadership point of view. *Mediterranean Journal of Social Sciences, 2*(3), 434-453. Retrieved from http://search.proquest.com/docview/1346960512?accountid=35812

Olasupo, M. O. (2011). Relationship between organizational cultures, leadership style and job satisfaction in a Nigerian manufacturing organization. *Ife PsychologIA, 19*(1), 159-176. Retrieved from http://search.proquest.com/docview/856362328?accountid=35812

Olu-Adeyemi. (2012). The challenges of democratic governance in Nigeria. *International Journal of Business and Social Science, 3*(5) Retrieved from http://search.proquest.com/docview/924459407?accountid=458

Ondercin, H. (2004). External validity. In M. Lewis-Beck, A. Bryman, & T. Liao (Eds.), *Encyclopedia of social science research methods.* (pp. 361-363). Thousand Oaks, CA: SAGE Publications, Inc. doi: http://dx.doi.org.ezproxy.apollolibrary.com/10.4135/9781412950589.n318

Orbe, M. (2009). Phenomenology. In S. Littlejohn, & K. Foss (Eds.), *Encyclopedia of communication theory.* (pp. 750-752). Thousand Oaks, CA: SAGE Publications, Inc. doi: http://dx.doi.org.ezproxy.apollolibrary.com/10.4135/9781412959384.n282

Ouchi, W. G. (1981). Organizational paradigms: a commentary on Japanese management and theory z organizations. *Organizational Dynamics, 9*(4), 36-43.

Osa-Afiana, L. (1996). Towards a new Nigeria. *Theweek.* Retrieved from http://search.proquest.com/docview/198920209?accountid=35812

Osteryoung J., (2008) Setting boundaries. *The Jim Moran institute for global entrepreneurship*; Retrieved from http://jmi.fsu.edu/Services/Jerry-s-Articles/How-to-Be-a-More-Effective-Manager/Setting-Boundaries

Parker, G. (2008). *Team players and teamwork: New strategies for developing successful collaboration, completely updated revised* (2nd Ed.). San Francisco, CA. Jossey-Bass.

Patton, Jr., G. S. (1978). *The Patton Principles.* Province Pub. Co (1978)

Patton, Jr., G. S. (1947) *War As I Knew It.* New York, New York: Houghton Mifflin Company.

Patton, M. Q. (2002). *Qualitative research & evaluation methods* (3rd edition). California: Sage Productions.

Patton, M. Q. (1990). *Qualitative evaluation and research methods* (2nd ed.). Newbury Park, CA: Sage.

Persaud, N. (2010). Pilot study. In N. Salkind (Ed.), E*ncyclopedia of research design.* (pp. 1033-1034). Thousand Oaks, CA: SAGE Publications, Inc. doi: http://dx.doi.org.ezproxy.apollolibrary.com/10.4135/9781412961288.n312

Philips D. and Esposito M. (2009). The similarities and differences between four leadership models and how they might address contemporary leadership issues and challenges. *Swiss Management Centre –University* (SMC-U). Retrieved from http://www.swissmc.ch/Media/Dexter_Philips_working_paper_04-2009.pdf

Plato (1988). *The laws of Plato.* T. Pangle (Trans.). Chicago: University of Chicago Press

Polgreen, L. (2007). Democracy in Nigeria falters but is far from dead. **New York Times** (1923-Current File). Retrieved from http://search.proquest --.com/docview/848088987?accountid=35812

Polinghorne, D. E. (1989). Phenomenological research methods. In R. S. Valle & s. Halling (Eds.), *Existential-phenomenological perspectives on psychology* (pp. 41-60). New York: Plenum.

Pollio, H. R., Henley, T. B., & Thompson, C. J. (1997). *The phenomenology of everyday life.* Cambridge: University Press.

Pospisil, Leopold J. (1958). Kapauku Papuan Political Structure. In *Systems of Political Control and Bureaucracy in Human Societies,* edited by Verne F. Ray. Seattle, WA: American Ethnological Society, pp. pp. 17–18.

Popper M. and Mayseless O. (2002). Internal world of transformational leaders. Bruce J Avolio; Francis J Yammarino, Transformational and charismatic leadership: the road ahead. Amsterdam; Boston: JAI, 2002. Series: *Monographs in leadership and management, v. 2.*

Porter, E. J. (1998). On "Being Inspired" by Husserl's Phenomenology: Reflections on Omery's exposition of phenomenology as a method of nursing research. Critique and Replication. *Advances in Nursing Science. 21*(1):16-28, September 1998.

Preissle, J. (2008). Ethics. In L. Given (Ed.), *The SAGE encyclopedia of qualitative research methods.* (pp. 274-278). Thousand Oaks, CA: SAGE Publications, Inc. doi: http://dx.doi.org.ezproxy.apollolibrary.com/10.4135/9781412963909.n140

Premeaux, S. (2009). The link between management behavior and ethical philosophy in the wake of the Enron convictions. *Journal of Business Ethics, 85*(1), 13-25.

Profile. (2011). Background Notes on Countries of the World: *Nigeria, 2.*

Rice, S. E. (1998). Prospects for democracy in Nigeria. *U.S. Department of State Dispatch, 9*(6), 12-14. Retrieved from http://search.proquest.com/docview/233224269?accountid=35812

Rosete, D., & Ciarrochi, J. (2005). Emotional intelligence and its relationship to workplace performance outcomes of leadership effectiveness. *Leadership & Organization Development Journal, 26*(5/6), 388.

Rossman, R. B., & Ralllis, S. F. (1998). *Learning in the field: An introduction to qualitative research.* Thousand Oaks, CA: Sage.

Rowold, J. and Schlotz, W. (2009). Transformational and transactional leadership and followers' chronic stress. Kravis Leadership Institute, *Leadership Review, Vol. 9,* spring 2009, pp. 35-48. Retrieved from http://www.leadershipreview.org/2009spring/article1.pdf

Rummler, G. A., & Brache, A. P. (2013). *Improving performance: How to manage the white space on the organizational chart* (3rd ed.). San Francisco, CA: Jossey-Bass.

Salkind N. J., (2002). Triangulation. In Calhoun, C. (Ed.), *Dictionary of the Social Sciences.* : Oxford University Press. Retrieved 14 Feb. 2014, from http://www.oxfordreference.com/view/10.1093/acref/9780195123715.001.0001/acref-9780195123715-e-1711.

Sales, B.D., & Folkman, S. (Eds.). (2000). Ethics in research with human participants. Washington, DC: *American Psychological Association.*

Santos, F. M., & Eisenhardt, K. M. (2005). Organizational boundaries and theories of organization. *Organization Science, 16*(5), 491-508. doi:10.1287/orsc.1050.0152. EBSCOHOST

Schaubroeck, J. M., Hannah, S. T., Avolio, B. J., Kozlowski, S. W., Lord, R. G., Trevinño, L. K., & Peng, A. C. (2012). Embedding ethical leadership within and across organization levels. *Academy of Management Journal, 55*(5), 1053-1078.

School of Advanced Studies, University of Phoenix. (2010). *Research and dissertation connectedness lecture.* [Class handout, DOC/721R Doctoral Seminar 1].

Schreiber, J. (2008). Pilot study. In L. Given (Ed.), *The SAGE encyclopedia of qualitative research methods.* (pp. 625-627). Thousand Oaks, CA: SAGE Publications, Inc. doi: http://dx.doi.org.ezproxy.apollolibrary.com/10.4135/9781412963909.n320

Schudlich, T., & Schudlich, J. (2008). Social development. In N. Salkind (Ed.), *Encyclopedia of educational psychology.* (pp. 913-920). Thousand Oaks, CA: SAGE Publications, Inc. doi: http://dx.doi.org.ezproxy.apollolibrary.com/10.4135/9781412963848.n251

Scott, W.R., Davis, G.F. (2007). *Organizations and organizing.* Upper Saddle River, NJ: Prentice Hall.

Seamon, D. (2010). *Phenomenology. In B. Warf (Ed.), Encyclopedia of geography.* (pp. 2166-2170). Thousand Oaks, CA: SAGE Publications, Inc. doi: http://dx.doi.org.ezproxy.apollolibrary.com/10.4135/9781412939591.n882

Seel R., (2006). Emergence in organizations. Retrieved from http://doingbetterthings.pbworks.com/f/RICHARD%2BSEEL%2BEmergence%2Bin%2BOrganisations.pdf paradigm.co.uk/

Shah, Iqbal, Razaq, Yameen, Sabir, & Khan (2011). Influential role of culture on leadership effectiveness and organizational performance. *Information Management and Business Review Vol. 3*, No. 2, pp. 127-132, Aug 2011 (ISSN 2220 -3796)

Shane, S. (2009). T*echnology strategy for managers, and entrepreneurs,* (1st Ed.). Upper Saddle River, NJ: Pearson.

Seidman I.E. (1991) *Interviewing as qualitative research.* Teachers College Press, New York.

Simon, M. K. (2006). *Dissertation & scholarly research: A practical guide to start & complete your dissertation, thesis, or formal research project.* Dubuque, IA: Kendall/Hunt Publishing Company.

Singh, N. (2011). Nigeria's elusive quest for democracy: multinational corporations and sustenance of authoritarianism. *African & Asian Studies, 10*(2/3), 209-233. doi: 10.1163/156921011X587031

Smith, S. (2010). Introduction. In S. Smith, R. Pain, S. Marston, & J. Jones (Eds.), *The sage handbook of social geographies.* (pp. 2-40). London: SAGE Publications Ltd. doi: http://dx.doi.org.ezproxy.apollolibrary.com/10.4135/9780857021113.n1

Sokoloski, R. (1999). I*ntroduction to phenomenology.* Cambridge: Cambridge University Press.

Stacks, D. (2005). Quantitative research. In R. Heath (Ed.), *Encyclopedia of public relations.* (pp. 729-732). Thousand Oaks, CA: SAGE Publications, Inc. doi: http://dx.doi.org.ezproxy.apollolibrary.com/10.4135/9781412952545.n364

Stogdill, R. M. (1948). Personal factors associated with leadership: A survey of the literature. *Journal of Psychology, 49*(1), 143.

Stogdill, R. M. (1995). Personal factors associated with leadership. In J.T. Wren (ed.), The leader's companion: Insights on leadership through the ages. New York: The Free Press. [Reprinted courtesy of the J*ournal of Contemporary Business, 3*(Autumn 1974).

Strauss, A. L., & Corbin, J. M. (1990). *Basics of qualitative research: Grounded theory procedures and techniques.* Newbury Park, CA: Sage Publications.

Strauss, A. L., & Corbin, J. M. (1998). *Basics of qualitative research: Techniques and procedures for developing grounded theory.* (2nd ed.). Thousand Oaks, CA: Sage Publications.

Suberu, R. T. (1994) *1991 state and local government reorganizations in Nigeria.* Institute of African Studies, University of Ibadan, Ibadan, Nigeria, ISBN 978-2015-28-8

SWOT Analysis. (2010). *Nigeria Oil & Gas Report, 9-10.*

Tajudeen, O. A., & Adebayo, F. O. (2013). Religious fanaticism and national security in Nigeria. *Journal of Sociological Research, 4*(1), 49-60. Retrieved from http://search.proquest.com/docview/1399039493?accountid=458

Taylor-Powel, E. & Hermann, C. (2000). Program development and evaluation, collecting evaluation data: *Surveys.* Retrieved from http://learningstore.uwex.edu/assets/pdfs/G3658-10.pdf

The United Nations Millennium Development Goals (2005). *Journal of International Affairs, 58*(2), 1

Thomas, C. (2005). External validity. In S. Mathison (Ed.), *Encyclopedia of evaluation.* (pp. 152-153). Thousand Oaks, CA: SAGE Publications, Inc. doi: http://dx.doi.org.ezproxy.apollolibrary.com/10.4135/9781412950558.n204

Thurmond, V. A. (2001). The point of triangulation. *Journal of Nursing Scholarship, 33*(3), 253-8. Retrieved from http://search.proquest.com/docview/236442422?accountid=458

Tichy N. M., and Devanna M. A. (1990). *The transformational leader: The Key to Global Competitiveness,* 1e John Wiley & Sons, Inc.

Tsai, Y. (2011). Relationship between organizational culture, leadership behavior and job satisfaction. *BMC Health Services Research 11* (2011): 98. Gale Power Search. Web. 14 August 2011.

Tymieniecka A. T. (Ed.). (2002). Phenomenology worldwide: Foundations, expanding dynamisms, life-engagements: A guide for research and study. Dordrecht, the Netherlands: *Kluwer Academic.*

Uche, C., Falola, Heaton, T., & Matthew. (2009). A history of Nigeria. *Journal of African History, 50*(1), 147-148. doi:http://dx.doi.org/10.1017/S0021853709004356

Udogu, E. (2009). A History of Nigeria. *Africa Today, 55*(4), 122-128.

United Nations Development Program (2013). The millennium development goals: Eight goals for 2015. Retrieved from http://www.undp.org/content/undp/en/home/mdgoverview/

Valentin, E. K. (2001). SWOT analysis from a resource-based view. Journal of Marketing *Theory and Practice, 9*(2), 54-69. Retrieved from http://search.proquest.com/docview/212164985?accountid=35812

van den Hoonaard, D., & van den Hoonaard, E. (2008). Data analysis. In L. Given (Ed.), *The SAGE encyclopedia of qualitative research methods.* (pp. 187-189). Thousand Oaks, CA: SAGE Publications, Inc. doi: http://dx.doi.org.ezproxy.apollolibrary.com/10.4135/9781412963909.n94

van den Hoonaard, Will C. (Ed.). (2002). *walking the tightrope: Ethical issues for qualitative researchers.* Toronto, ON: University of Toronto Press.

Van Manen, J. (1990). *Researching lived experience: Human science for an action sensitive pedagogy.* Albany: State University of New York Press.

van Teijlingen, E., & Hundley, V. (2004). Pilot study. In M. Lewis-Beck, A. Bryman, & T. Liao (Eds.), *Encyclopedia of social science research methods.* (pp. 824-825). Thousand Oaks, CA: SAGE Publications, Inc. doi: http://dx.doi.org.ezproxy.apollolibrary.com/10.4135/9781412950589.n715

von Ecksberg, R. (1998). Introducing existential-phenomenological psychology. In R. Valle (Ed.), *Phenomenological inquiry in psychology: Existential and transpersonal dimensions* (pp. 157-174). New York: Plenum.

Vroom, Victor H.; Jago, Arthur G. (1988). *The new leadership: Managing participation in organizations.* Englewood Cliffs, NJ: Prentice-Hall. ISBN 0-13-615030-6.

Vroom, Victor H.; Yetton, Phillip W. (1973). *Leadership and Decision-Making.* Pittsburgh: University of Pittsburgh Press. ISBN 0-8229-3266-0.

Waskey, A. (2008). Ethics. In C. Svendsen, & A. Ebert (Eds.), *Encyclopedia of stem cell research.* (pp. 190-194). Thousand Oaks, CA: SAGE Publications, Inc. doi: http://dx.doi.org.ezproxy.apollolibrary.com/10.4135/9781412963954.n89

Waterstone, M. (2010). Geography and social justice. In S. Smith, R. Pain, S. Marston, & J. Jones (Eds.), *The Sage Handbook of Social Geographies.* (Vol. 12, pp. 419-435). London: SAGE Publications Ltd. doi: http://dx.doi.org.ezproxy.apollolibrary.com/10.4135/9780857021113.n19

Weiss, R. S. (1994). *Learning from strangers: The art and method of qualitative interview studies.* New York: Free Press.

Whitley, R. & Crawford, M. (2005). Qualitative research in psychiatry. *Canadian Journal of Psychiatry, 50*(2), 108-114. Retrieved from EBSCOhost database.

Willis, J. W. (2007). *Foundations of qualitative research: Interpretive and critical approaches.* Thousand Oaks, CA: Sage.

Wren, J.T. (1995). The leader's companion: *Insights on leadership through the ages.* New York: The Free Press. [Reprinted courtesy of the *Journal of Contemporary Business, 3*(Autumn 1974) published by the School of Business Administration, University of Washington, Seattle, WA.

Xenias, A. (2008). Economy. In K. Warren (Ed.), *Encyclopedia of U.S. Campaigns, Elections, and Electoral Behavior.* (pp. 191-193). Thousand Oaks, CA: SAGE Publications, Inc. doi: http://dx.doi.org.ezproxy.apollolibrary.com/10.4135/9781412963886.n94

Yin, R. K. (2010). *Qualitative research from start to finish.* Guilford Press.

Yukl, G. (2006, 2010). *Leadership in organizations* (7th Ed.). Upper Saddle River, NJ. Pearson Prentice Hall History. (2008).

APPENDIX A: INFORMED CONSENT

Date: ___________

Dear ___________,

[redacted] I am doing a research study entitled *"A phenomenological study of the influence of Nigerian leadership on the life of its citizens."* The purpose of the research study is to specifically understand how political, cultural, social and economic conditions in Nigeria influence the lives of Nigerian citizens through lived experiences of two citizens from each of the six geopolitical regions of the country namely, North-Central, North-Eastern, North-Western, South-Eastern, South-South, and South-Western regions..

Your participation will involve a face-to-face interview and you will be asked open-ended questions about your experience of living under economic, political, cultural, and social structure in Nigeria. Interviews will be approximately 60 -90 minutes in length. Participation in the study is on a voluntary basis. If you wish to withdraw from the study, you can do so without penalty. The results of the study may be published but your identity will remain confidential and your name will not be disclosed to any outside party. You can decide to be a part of this study or not. Once you start, you can withdraw from the study at any time without any penalty or loss of benefits. The results of the research study may be published but your identity will remain confidential and your name will not be made known to any outside party.

In this research, there are no foreseeable risks to you. Although there may be no direct benefit to you, a possible benefit from your being part of this study is that your efforts would go into records as being a part of a qualitative phenomenological study on critical factors that contribute to the leadership problems in Nigeria. A completed work would be offered to you as a souvenir. If you have any questions about the research study, please call me at 281-546-3333 or email – anthony@guardiannews.us.

For questions about your rights as a study participant, or any concerns or complaints, please contact the University of Phoenix Institutional Review Board via email at IRB@phoenix.edu.

As a participant in this study, you should understand the following:

1. You may decide not to be part of this study or you may want to withdraw from the study at any time. If you want to withdraw, you can do so without any problems.
2. Your identity will be kept confidential.
3. Anthony Ogbo, the researcher, has fully explained the nature of the research study and has answered all of your questions and concerns.
4. If interviews are done, they may be recorded. If they are recorded, you must give permission for the researcher, Anthony Ogbo, to record the interviews. You understand that the information from the recorded interviews may be transcribed. The researcher will develop a way to code the data to assure that your name is protected.
5. Data will be kept in a secure and locked area. The data will be kept for three years, and then destroyed.
6. The results of this study may be published.

"By signing this form, you agree that you understand the nature of the study, the possible risks to you as a participant, and how your identity will be kept confidential. When you sign this form, this means that you are 18 years old or older and that you give your permission to volunteer as a participant in the study that is described here."

(☐) I accept the above terms. (☐) I do not accept the above terms. (CHECK ONE)

Signature of the interviewee ______________________________ Date ___________

Signature of the researcher ______________________________ Date ___________

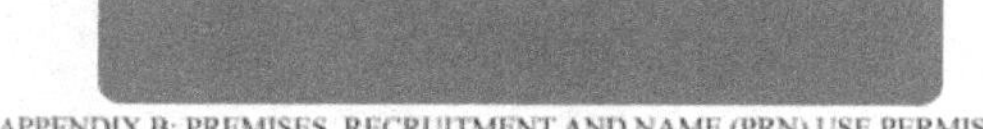

APPENDIX B: PREMISES, RECRUITMENT AND NAME (PRN) USE PERMISSION

02/29/2015

Check all that apply:

___ I hereby authorize Anthony Ogbo, to use the premises (facility identified below) to conduct a study entitled: A phenomenological study of the influence of Nigerian leadership on the life of its citizens.

___ I hereby authorize Anthony Ogbo to recruit subjects for participation to conduct a study entitled: A phenomenological study of the influence of Nigerian leadership on the life of its citizens.

___ I hereby authorize Anthony Ogbo, to use the name of the facility, organization, university, institution, or association identified above when publishing results from the study entitled: A phenomenological study of the influence of Nigerian leadership on the life of its citizens.

Signature ______________ Date 2/25/15

Name ______________ Title ______________

APPENDIX C: INTERVIEW PROTOCOL

To carry out the interviews I plan to:

1. Mail or hand over the consent form to participants and obtain consent for the study.
2. Schedule participant interviews and discuss consent, confidentiality, recording of interview.
3. Arrive 10-15 minutes early at each interview site.
4. Respectfully and professionally greet each interview participant through a brief introduction of myself.
5. Gather written consent from participant and begin interviews.
6. Record each interview session and indicate time, place, date, and participant.
7. Begin the conversation by introducing interview questions.
8. Summarize main themes to confirm accuracy of the interview responses.
9. Conclude interview session and answer any potential questions from the participant.
10. Press stop on the recorder, and graciously thank the participant for taking part in the interview.

APPENDIX D: INTERVIEW QUESTIONS

The purpose of the qualitative phenomenological research study is to understand how political, cultural, social and economic conditions in Nigeria influence the lives of Nigerian citizens through lived experiences of two citizens from each of the six geopolitical regions of the country namely, North-Central, North-Eastern, North-Western, South-Eastern, South-South, and South-Western regions. This interview will specifically focus on your experience as a Nigerian living in Nigeria, under economic, political, cultural, and social hardships. Think about what you experience as a Nigerian living in Nigeria under various regimes you have lived through; think about your experience having lived through the economic, political, social, and cultural system; think about the leaders who led through those regimes, and how their economic, political, social, and cultural system policies or management have influenced your livelihood. This interview will try to uncover the array of cognitive phases that you have experienced.

Questions

1. What does being a Nigerian citizen mean to you?
2. Please, describe how you feel about your government?
3. Please, describe how you feel about your leaders?
4. How is the leadership in Nigeria affecting the quality of your life as a citizen?
5. Please describe how you feel about the political process in Nigeria?
6. How is the political process affecting the quality of your life as a citizen?
7. Please describe how you feel about the economic process in Nigeria?
8. How is the economic process affecting the quality of your life as a citizen?
9. Please describe how you feel about the social process in Nigeria?
10. How is the social process affecting the quality of your life as a citizen?
11. Please describe how you feel about the cultural process in Nigeria?
12. How is the cultural process affecting the quality of your life as a citizen?
13. Before we conclude this interview, what else would you like to share about your experience of living in Nigeria as a Nigerian Citizen?

Demographic Inquiries

Gender __ (M) __ (F)

Participants' Identification	NC-1 ☐	NW-1 ☐	SS-1 ☐
	NC-2 ☐	NW-2 ☐	SS-2 ☐
	NE-1 ☐	SE-1 ☐	SW-1 ☐
	NE-2 ☐	SE-2 ☐	SW-2 ☐

Age Range	30-35 ☐	41-45 ☐	56-60 ☐
	36-40 ☐	46-50 ☐	66-70 ☐
	41-45 ☐	51-55 ☐	71-75 ☐

Geographical Zone	N-C ☐	S-E ☐
	N-E ☐	S-S ☐
	N-W ☐	S-W ☐

Doctor of Management, Anthony Obi Ogbo is the publisher of Houston-based International Guardian, and the Author of *"Out of Texas: 336 Hours in Motherland,"* a book on politics, leadership, and psychology. A former president of Houston Association of Black Journalists with several merit awards to his credit, Ogbo started his media career in 1981 and has worked in various print media companies until 1998 when inaugurated the *International Guardian.* Ogbo holds a degree in Fine & Applied Arts; a certificate in Commercial Arts; a Masters in Human Resources and Human Resources Management, and doctorate in the esoteric field of Management in Organizational Leadership. Ogbo print media activities had been limited by a current transition to the college system. He is currently the founder and the Chancellor of *American Journal of Transformational Leadership* – a nonprofit educational and research entity, with the core mission to inspire the study of management and organizational leadership in the society, nationally and internationally.

www.ingramcontent.com/pod-product-compliance
Lightning Source LLC
Chambersburg PA
CBHW030435290526
45786CB00001B/290

* 9 7 8 1 5 1 5 2 3 8 2 7 0 *